ALSO BY JOHN GRAY

Mill on Liberty: A Defense

Conceptions of Liberty in Political Philosophy
(ed. with Zbigniew Pelczynski)

Hayek on Liberty

Liberalism

Liberalisms: Essays in Political Philosophy

J. S. Mill, "On Liberty": In Focus (ed. with G. W. Smith)

*Beyond the New Right: Markets,
Government and the Common Environment*

Post-Liberalism: Studies in Political Thought

*Enlightenment's Wake:
Politics and Culture at the Close of the Modern Age*

Isaiah Berlin

After Social Democracy: Politics, Capitalism and the Common Life

Endgames: Questions in Late Modern Political Thought

False Dawn: The Delusions of Global Capitalism

Voltaire

Two Faces of Liberalism

Al Qaeda and What It Means to Be Modern

Heresies: Against Progress and Other Illusions

Black Mass: Apocalyptic Religion and the Death of Utopia

Straw Dogs: Thoughts on Humans and Other Animals

*The Immortalization Commission:
Science and the Strange Quest to Cheat Death*

THE SILENCE OF ANIMALS

THE SILENCE OF ANIMALS

ON PROGRESS AND OTHER MODERN MYTHS

JOHN GRAY

FARRAR, STRAUS AND GIROUX   NEW YORK

Farrar, Straus and Giroux
18 West 18th Street, New York 10011

Originally published in 2013 by Allen Lane, an imprint of Penguin
Books, Great Britain
Published in the United States in 2013 by Farrar, Straus and Giroux
First American paperback edition, 2014

Owing to limitations of space, all acknowledgements
for permission to reprint previously published material
can be found on pages 227–228.

Library of Congress Control Number: 2013936278
ISBN: 978-0-374-22917-7
Paperback ISBN: 978-0-374-53466-0

Farrar, Straus and Giroux books may be purchased for educational,
business, or promotional use. For information on bulk purchases,
please contact the Macmillan Corporate and Premium Sales
Department at 1-800-221-7945, extension 5442, or write to
specialmarkets@macmillan.com.

www.fsgbooks.com
www.twitter.com/fsgbooks • www.facebook.com/fsgbooks

1   3   5   7   9   10   8   6   4   2

The seasons are no longer what they once were,
But it is the nature of things to be seen only once,
As they happen along . . .

John Ashbery

Contents

THE SILENCE OF ANIMALS

1 An Old Chaos

The highly civilized apes swung gracefully from bough to bough; the Neanderthaler was uncouth and bound to the earth. The apes, saturated and playful, lived in sophisticated playfulness, or caught fleas in philosophic contemplation; the Neanderthaler trampled gloomily through the world, banging around with clubs. The apes looked down on him amusedly from their tree tops and threw nuts at him. Sometimes horror seized them: they ate fruits and tender plants with delicate refinement; the Neanderthaler devoured raw meat, he slaughtered animals and his fellows. He cut down trees that had always stood, moved rocks from their time-hallowed place, transgressed every law and tradition of the jungle. He was uncouth, cruel, without animal dignity – from the point of view of the highly civilized apes, a barbaric relapse of history.

Arthur Koestler, *Darkness at Noon*

THE CALL OF PROGRESS

'Kayerts was hanging by a leather strap from the cross. He had evidently climbed the grave, which was high and narrow, and after tying the end of the strap to the arm, had swung himself off. His toes were only a couple of inches above the ground: his arms hung stiffly down; he seemed to be standing rigidly at attention; but with one purple cheek playfully posed on the shoulder. And, irreverently, he was putting out a swollen tongue at his Managing Director.'

The hanged man was one of a pair of traders sent by a Belgian corporation to a remote part of the Congo, 300 miles away from the nearest trading post. Most of their work was done by a native interpreter, who used a visit by some tribesmen to sell some of the outpost's workers as slaves in exchange for ivory tusks. Initially shocked at being involved in slave-trading but finding the deal highly profitable, Kayerts and the other European Carlier accepted the trade. Having made the deal, they were left with little to occupy their time. They passed their days reading cheap novels and old newspapers extolling 'Our Colonial Expansion' and 'the merits of those who went about bringing light, faith and commerce to the dark places of the earth'. Reading these newspapers, Carlier and Kayerts 'began to think better of them-selves'. Over the next few months they lost the habit of work. The steamer they were expecting did not come and their supplies began to run out. Quarrelling over some lumps of sugar that Kayerts held in reserve, Carlier was killed. In desperation, Kayerts decided to kill himself too. As he was hanging himself on the cross, the steamer arrived. When the Managing Director disembarks, he finds himself face to face with the dead Kayerts.

Joseph Conrad wrote 'An Outpost of Progress' in 1896, and it is a story at least as ferocious and disabused as his later and better-known novella *Heart of Darkness*. Conrad describes how Kayerts 'sat by the corpse [of Carlier] thinking; thinking very actively, thinking very new thoughts. His old thoughts, convictions, likes and dislikes, things he respected and things he abhorred, appeared in their true light at last! Appeared contemptible and childish, false and ridiculous. He revelled in his new wisdom while he sat by the man he had killed.' But not all of Kayerts's old convictions have vanished, and what he still believes in leads him to his death. 'Progress was calling Kayerts from the river. Progress and civilisation and all the virtues. Society was calling to its accomplished child to come to be taken care of, to be instructed, to be judged, to be condemned; it called him to return from that rubbish heap from which he had wandered away, so that justice could be done.'

In setting his tale in the Congo, where he had

observed the effects of Belgian imperialism at first hand when he visited the country in 1890 to take command of a river steamer, Conrad was making use of a change he had himself undergone. Arriving with the conviction that he was a civilized human being, he realized what in fact he had been: 'Before the Congo, I was just a mere animal.' The animal to which Conrad refers was European humanity, which caused the deaths of millions of human beings in the Congo.

The idea that imperialism could be a force for human advance has long since fallen into disrepute. But the faith that was once attached to empire has not been renounced. Instead it has spread everywhere. Even those who nominally follow more traditional creeds rely on a belief in the future for their mental composure. History may be a succession of absurdities, tragedies and crimes; but – everyone insists – the future can still be better than anything in the past. To give up this hope would induce a state of despair like that which unhinged Kayerts.

Among the many benefits of faith in progress the most important may be that it prevents too much self-knowledge. When Kayerts and his companion ventured into the Congo the aliens they met were not the indigenous inhabitants but themselves.

They lived like blind men in a large room, aware only of what came in contact with them (and of that only imperfectly), but unable to see the general aspect of things. The river, the forest, all the great land throbbing with life, were like a great emptiness. Things appeared and disappeared before their eyes in an unconnected and aimless kind of way. The river flowed through a void. Out of that void, at times, came canoes, and men with spears in their hands would suddenly crowd the yard of the station.

They cannot endure the silence into which they have come: 'stretching away in all directions, surrounding the insignificant cleared spot of the trading post, immense forests, hiding fateful complications of fantastic life, lay in the eloquent silence of mute greatness.' The sense of the progression of time, which they had brought with them, begins to fall away. As Conrad writes towards the end of the story, 'Those fellows, having engaged themselves to the Company for six months (without having any idea of a month in particular and only a very faint notion of time in general), had been serving the cause of progress for upwards of two years.' Removed from their habits, Kayerts and Carlier lose the abilities that are needed to go on living. 'Society, not from any tenderness, but because of its strange needs, had taken care of those two men, forbidding them all independent thought, all initiative, all departure from routine; and forbidding it under pain of death. They could live only on condition of being machines.'

The machine-like condition of modern humans may seem a limitation. In fact it is a condition of their survival. Kayerts and Carlier were able to function as individuals only because they had been shaped by society down to their innermost being. They were:

> two perfectly insignificant and incapable individuals, whose existence is only rendered possible through the high organization of civilized crowds. Few men realize that their life, the very essence of their character, their capabilities and their audacities, are only the expression of their belief in the safety of their surroundings. The courage, the composure, the confidence; the emotions and principles; every great and every insignificant thought belongs not to the individual but to the crowd: to the crowd that believes blindly in the irresistible force of its institutions and of its morals, in the power of the police and of its opinion.

When they stepped outside of their normal surroundings, the two men were powerless to act. More than that: they ceased to exist.

For those who live inside a myth, it seems a self-evident fact. Human progress is a fact of this kind. If you accept it you have a place in the grand march of humanity. Humankind is, of course, not marching anywhere. 'Humanity' is a fiction composed from billions of individuals for each of whom life is singular and final. But the myth of progress is extremely potent. When it loses its power those who have lived by it are – as Conrad put it, describing Kayerts and Carlier – 'like those lifelong prisoners who, liberated after many years, do not know what use to make of their freedoms'. When faith in the future is taken from them, so is the image they have of themselves. If they then opt for death, it is because without that faith they can no longer make sense of living.

When Kayerts decides to end his life he does it by hanging himself on a cross. 'Kayerts stood still. He looked upwards; the fog rolled low over his head. He looked around like a man who has lost his way; and he saw a dark smudge, a cross-shaped stain, upon the shifting purity of the mist. As he began to stumble towards it, the station bell rang in a tumultuous peal its answer to the impatient clamour of the steamer.' Just as the steamer is arriving – showing that civilization is still intact – Kayerts reaches the cross, where he finds redemption in death.

What has the cross to do with progress? Conrad tells us that it had been put up by the Director of the Great Trading Company to mark the grave of the first of his agents, formerly an unsuccessful painter, who 'had planned and had watched the construction of this outpost of progress'. The cross was 'much out of the perpendicular', causing Carlier to squint whenever he passed it, so one day he replants it upright. Wanting to make sure that it is solid, he applies his weight to it: 'I suspended myself with both hands to the cross-piece. Not a move. Oh, I did that properly.' It is on this tall, sturdy structure, which appears to him as a dark, smudged stain in the mist, that Kayerts ends his life.

In the story that the modern world repeats to itself, the belief in progress is at odds with religion. In the dark ages of faith there was no hope of any fundamental change in human life. With the arrival of modern science, a vista of improvement opened up. Increasing knowledge allowed humans to take control of their destiny. From being lost in the shadows, they could step out into the light.

In fact the idea of progress is not at odds with religion in the way this modern fairy tale suggests. Faith in progress is a late survival of early Christianity, originating in the message of Jesus, a dissident Jewish prophet who announced the end of time. For the ancient Egyptians as for the ancient Greeks, there was nothing new under the sun. Human history belongs in the cycles of the natural world. The same is true in Hinduism and Buddhism, Daoism and Shinto, and the older parts of the Hebrew Bible. By creating the expectation of a radical alteration in human affairs, Christianity – the religion that St Paul invented from Jesus' life and sayings – founded the modern world.

In practice human beings continued to live much as they had always done. As Wallace Stevens wrote:

> She hears, upon that water without sound,
> A voice that cries, 'The tomb in Palestine
> Is not the porch of spirits lingering,
> It is the grave of Jesus, where he lay.'
> We live in an old chaos of the sun.

It was not long before a literal expectation of the End was turned into a metaphor for a spiritual transformation. Yet a change had taken place in what was hoped of the future. Many transmutations were needed before the Christian story could renew itself as the myth of progress. But from being a succession of cycles like the seasons, history came to be seen as a story of redemption and salvation, and in modern times salvation became identified with the increase of knowledge and power – the myth that took Kayerts and Carlier to the Congo.

When Conrad used his experiences of the Congo in *Heart of Darkness* (1899), he was not telling a story of barbarism in faraway places. The narrator tells the tale on a yacht moored in the Thames estuary: barbarism is not a primitive form of life, Conrad is intimating, but a pathological development of civilization. The same thought recurs in *The Secret Agent* (1907), Conrad's novel of terrorism and conspiracy, which is set in London. The anarchist Professor, who travels everywhere with a bomb in his coat that he intends to detonate if arrested, wants to believe that humanity has been corrupted by government, an essentially criminal institution. But, as Conrad understood, it is not only government that is tainted by criminality. All human institutions – families and churches, police forces and anarchists – are stained by crime. Explaining human nastiness by reference to corrupt institutions leaves a question: why are humans so attached to corruption? Clearly, the answer is in the human animal itself.

Conrad shows the Professor struggling with this truth: 'He was in a long, straight street, peopled by a mere fraction of an immense multitude; but all around him, on and on, even to the limits of the horizon hidden by the enormous piles of bricks, he felt the mass of mankind mighty in its numbers. They swarmed numerous like locusts, industrious like ants, thoughtless like a natural force, pushing on blind and orderly and absorbed, impervious to sentiment, to logic, to terror too, perhaps.'

The Professor continues to dream of a future in which humans will be regenerated. But what he truly loves is destruction: 'the incorruptible Professor walked, averting his eyes from the odious multitude. He had no future. He disdained it. He was a force. His thoughts caressed the images of ruin and destruction. He walked frail, insignificant, shabby, miserable – and terrible in the simplicity of his idea calling madness and despair to the regeneration of the world.' If Kayerts hanged himself because he no longer believed in progress, the Professor is ready to kill and die in order to show that he still has faith in the future.

The myth of progress casts a glimmer of meaning into the lives of those who accept it. Kayerts, Carlier and many like them did nothing that could be described as significant. But their faith in progress allowed their petty schemes to seem part of a grand design, while their miserable deaths achieved a kind of exemplary futility their lives had not possessed.

FROZEN HORSES AND DESERTS OF BRICK

When Norman Lewis arrived in Naples as an officer of the British Intelligence Corps in early October 1943 he found a city on the brink of starvation.

It is astonishing to witness the struggles of this city so shattered, so starved, so deprived of all those things that justify a city's existence, to adapt itself to a collapse into conditions which must resemble life in the Dark Ages. People camp out like Bedouins in deserts of brick. There is little food, little water, no salt, no soap. A lot of Neapolitans have lost their possessions, including most of their clothing, in the bombings, and I have seen some strange combinations of garments about the streets, including a man in an old dinner jacket, knickerbockers and army boots and several women in lacy confections that might have been made up from curtains. There are no cars but carts by the hundred, and a few antique coaches such as barouches and phaetons drawn by lean horses. Today at Posilippo I stopped to watch the methodical dismemberment of a stranded German half-track by a number of youths who were streaming away from it like leaf-cutter ants, carrying pieces of metal of all shapes and sizes . . . Everyone improvises and adapts.

In the book he wrote about his experiences, *Naples '44*, published in 1978, Lewis presents a picture of life as it is lived when civilization has crumbled. Hit by plague – a typhus epidemic visited the city not long after its liberation, while syphilis was rampant – the inhabitants were surrounded by death and disease. Beyond the struggle against sickness, there was another struggle that was all-consuming – the daily effort simply to stay alive.

Lewis's life was driven by an impulse to escape the restrictions of interwar England. Born and passing most of his early years in the London suburb of Enfield, he married the daughter of a member of the Sicilian mafia who had ended up in Bloomsbury. Having been smuggled into America in a coffin, Lewis's future father-in-law decided to return to Europe after his New York apartment was machine-gunned. It seems to have been the Sicilian who funded Lewis's excursion into business as the owner of the photography shop R. G. Lewis, through which Lewis would for a time corner the British market in Leica cameras. According to Lewis, it was through an encounter in this shop that he was recruited as an 'amateur spy' by British intelligence in 1937 and sent on a mission to Yemen, travelling there by dhow only to be refused entry to the still-feudal country. On the way home he was befriended by an English archaeologist, who seems to have been responsible for Lewis joining the Intelligence Corps.

When Lewis landed in September 1943 on the beach at Paestum, south-east of Naples, he found that 'an extraordinary false serenity lay on the land-ward view'. The beach was covered by corpses, 'laid out in a row, side by side, shoulder to shoulder, with extreme precision as if about to present arms at an inspection by death'. Inland, with the sun sinking into the sea at his back, Lewis came on 'the three perfect temples of Paestum, pink and glowing and glorious in the sun's last rays'. In the field between him and the temple were two dead cows, their feet in the air. Lewis writes that the sight came to him 'as an illumination, one of the great experiences of life'.

As Lewis records, when Naples was liberated by the Allies the entire population was out of work and foraging for food. Liberation was preceded by carpet-bombing in which working-class districts were destroyed and electricity and water supplies cut off. Delayed-action bombs left by the retreating Germans added to the dangers. With no functioning economy the inhabitants scavenged for whatever was left, including tropical fish in the city aquarium. Thousands of people crammed into a single acre lived on scraps of offal from slaughterhouses, fishes' heads and cats caught in the street. Families searched for mushrooms and dandelions in the countryside and set up traps to catch birds. Ignored by the Allied administration, there was a thriving black market in medicines.

With everything on sale, anything that could be moved – statues from public squares, telegraph poles, phials of penicillin and medical instruments, small boats, tombstones, petrol, tyres, the contents of museums, the bronze doors of a cathedral – was liable to be stolen. Formerly middle-class people hawked jewellery, books and paintings, a 'white-lipped and

smiling' priest sold umbrellas, candlesticks and orna-
ments carved from bones stolen from the catacombs,
while around a third of the city's women were selling
sex on an occasional or regular basis. Lewis reports
the visit to him of a local prince, owner of a nearby
palace and absentee landlord of a vast estate, who
had fallen on hard times. The prince served as an
informant, but in this case he came with his sister to
discuss finding a place for her in a military brothel.
When Lewis explained that the British army did not
have such an institution, the prince was at a loss. 'A
pity,' he said. Then, turning to his sister who like him
spoke perfect English, the prince commiserated: 'Ah
well, Luisa, I suppose if it can't be, it can't be.'

Such law and order as existed was provided by
the Camorra. Having evolved as 'a system of self-
protection against the bullies and the tax-collectors
of a succession of foreign governments', the organization was now not much more than a racket. The
police and the courts were thoroughly corrupt.
Hoping to impose some limits on the black market,
Lewis decided to arrest a racketeer involved in smug-
gling penicillin. 'Dapper and imperturbable', the
racketeer told Lewis: 'This will do you no good. Who
are you? You are no one. I was dining with a certain
colonel last night. If you are tired of life in Naples, I
can have you sent away.' The racketeer was taken in,
and when Lewis visited him in his cell he found the

smuggler enjoying a fine meal, which he invited Lewis to share. The case made no progress. The witness Lewis expected to testify refused to appear, and the racketeer was found to have ailments that required him to stay in a hospital. In effect he was beyond justice. When Lewis reported the situation to his superiors he was told they were surprised he could spare the time to pursue the matter.

Lewis came to see his attempts to inject a semblance of justice into the city as pointless, even harmful. 'The fact is that we have upset the balance of nature here. I personally have been rigid when I should have been flexible. Here the police – corrupt and tyrannical as they are – and the civil population play a game together, but the rules are complex and I do not understand them, and through lack of understanding I lose respect.' Lewis also wrote *The Honoured Society: The Sicilian Mafia Observed* (1964), a not unsympathetic study of the criminal organization.

In the conditions Lewis witnessed in Naples, morality no longer applied. Writing in his autobiography *I Came, I Saw* (1985) he tells of Soviet prisoners of war who managed to reach the city, where they were interned and then put on a troop ship. Lewis discovered how they had survived German captivity.

I spent many hours listening to these ultimate survivors' experiences, and came to know that for every Soviet who had come through the fiery furnace of the POW camps, a hundred had found a miserable death. One survivor, a nineteen year old Tadjik herdsman who had been among those rounded up and put into camps, recalled being addressed in Russian through a loud-hailer by a short, bespectacled, mild-mannered German, who told the prisoners: 'There are far more of you than expected. We have food for 1,000 and there are 10,000 of you here, so you must draw your own conclusions.'

As Lewis recounted, for the survivors, emerging from camps in which four or five million had perished, 'the first hurdle to be cleared was an aversion to cannibalism; and I learnt that all of the men on this ship had eaten human flesh. The majority admitted to this without hesitation, often, surprisingly – as if the confession provided psychological release – with a kind of eagerness. Squatting in the fetid twilight below deck they would describe, as if relating some grim old Asian fable, the screaming, clawing scrambles that sometimes happened when a man died, when the prisoners fought like ravenous dogs to gorge themselves on the corpse before the Germans could drag it away.'

Having survived the German camps and then served in the German army, the prisoners of war dreaded being repatriated to the Soviets. Their fears were calmed when they persuaded the British to kit them out in khaki. Wearing British uniforms, the prisoners believed, would ensure that they were treated by the Soviet authorities as allies. Suspecting that the future of the prisoners would not be benign, the British chose not to inquire too closely into their fate. In the event, when the hand-over took place most of the ultimate survivors were shot and the rest consigned to the gulag.

As a result of his time in Naples Lewis underwent a conversion. The experience occurred when a group of girls between the ages of nine and twelve appeared in the doorway of a restaurant where he was eating. The girls were orphans, attracted to the restaurant by the smell of food. Noticing that they were weeping and realizing they were blind, he expected his fellow diners to interrupt their meal. But nobody moved. The girls were treated as though they did not exist. 'Forkfuls of food were thrust into open mouths, the rattle of conversation continued, nobody saw the tears.'

Reflecting on the scene Lewis found 'the experience changed my outlook. Until now I had clung to the comforting belief that human beings eventually come to terms with pain and sorrow. Now I understood I was wrong, and like Paul I suffered a conversion – but to pessimism . . . I knew that, condemned to everlasting darkness, hunger and loss, they would weep incessantly. They would never recover from their pain, and I would never recover from the memory of it.'

Lewis's conversion did not lessen his enjoyment of life. In later years he professed to be interested chiefly in growing lilies, producing some of the rarest in England. But he continued to travel widely. Whether they deal with the destruction of the ancient civilizations of South-east Asia by decades of war or the enslavement by Christian missionaries of traditional peoples in the Amazon, the books he went on to produce during his long life (he died in 2003 at the age of ninety-five) reveal an enduring melancholy mixed with what he described as 'the intense joy I feel from being alive'.

Life in Naples in 1944 did not change Curzio Malaparte as it had changed Lewis. A writer and soldier, architect and composer, press co-ordinator at the Versailles peace conference in 1919, author of a manual on the technique of the *coup d'état* that is still being consulted today, Malaparte found himself in Naples at the same time as Lewis, who reported catching a glimpse of his 'haunted face' at a party on the nearby island of Capri. Soon after arriving in Naples, Malaparte offered his services to the liberators and secured a position acting as Italian liaison officer with the American High Command. Around the same time he seems to have become an American intelligence asset.

For Malaparte the fight for life after the city was liberated was worse than anything that went on during the war:

> Before the liberation we had fought and suffered in order *not to die*. Now we were fighting and suffering *in order to live*. There is a profound difference between fighting to avoid death and fighting in order to live. Men who fight to avoid death preserve their dignity and one and all – men, women and children – defend it jealously, tenaciously, fiercely . . . When men fight to avoid death they cling with a tenacity born of desperation to all that constitutes the living and eternal part of human life, the essence, the noblest and purest element of life: dignity, pride, freedom of conscience. They fight to save their souls. But after the liberation men had to fight *in order to live* . . . It is a humiliating, horrible thing, a shameful necessity, a fight for life. Only for life. Only to save one's skin.

Observing the struggle for life in the city, Malaparte watched as civilization gave way. The people the inhabitants had imagined themselves to be – shaped, however imperfectly, by ideas of right and wrong – disappeared. What were left were hungry animals, ready to do anything to go on living; but not animals of the kind that innocently kill and die in forests and jungles. Lacking a self-image of the sort humans cherish, other animals are content to be what they are. For human beings the struggle for survival is a struggle against themselves.

Malaparte called the book in which he recounted his period in Naples *The Skin*. Appearing in 1949, it was placed on the Vatican's index of prohibited books – and not without reason. If the Neapolitans suffered less than other Europeans when civilization failed, Malaparte claimed, it was because they had never been in any deep sense Christian. The religion that conquered Europe was accepted by them in a superficial way, as a continuation of older cults. It did not enter their souls. As a result, he believed, it was easier for them to relinquish their self-image as moral beings.

A surrealist portrayal of the author's experiences rather than a literal account of events, *The Skin* reports conversations the author imagines having had with the city's American liberators. In one of them he speaks lyrically of the uniqueness of Naples: 'Naples is the most mysterious city in Europe. It is the only city of the ancient world that has not perished like Nineveh, Ilium or Babylon. It is the only city in the world that did not founder in the colossal shipwreck of ancient civilization. Naples is a Pompeii that was never buried. It is not a city: it is a world –

the ancient, pre-Christian world – that has survived intact on the surface of the modern world.'

As Malaparte saw it, Naples was a pagan city with an ancient sense of time. Christianity taught those who were converted to it to think of history as the unfolding of a single plot – a moral drama of sin and redemption. In the ancient world there was no such plot – only a multitude of stories that were forever being repeated. Inhabiting that ancient world, the Neapolitans did not expect any fundamental alteration in human affairs. Not having accepted the Christian story of redemption, they had not been seduced by the myth of progress. Never having believed civilization to be permanent, they were not surprised when it foundered.

If we are to believe him, the sight of Naples in ruins did not induce in Malaparte melancholy of the kind it left in Lewis. Instead the spectacle invigorated him. In *Kaputt*, his semi-fictional account of his travels in Nazi-occupied Europe published in 1944, Malaparte wrote:

I had never felt so close to the people – I – who until then had always felt a stranger in Naples: I had never felt so close to the crowd which until that day had felt so alien and different. I was covered with dust and sweat, my uniform was torn, my face unshaven, my hands and face greasy and soiled. I had come out of prison only a few hours before and found in that crowd a human warmth, a human affection, a human companionship, distress of the same kind as my own, but only greater, deeper and perhaps more real and ancient than my own. A suffering rendered sacred by its age, its fatalism, its mysterious nature, compared with which my own suffering was only human, new and without any deep roots in my own age. A suffering bereft of despair, and lighted by a great, beautiful hope, compared with which my own poor and small despair was merely a puny feeling that made me ashamed.

If Malaparte's sorrow was slight compared with that of the Neapolitans, the reason may have been that he took care he did not suffer as they did. In *Kaputt* he portrays himself as a dissident, mocking his Nazi hosts as he drinks and dines with them all over Europe. In fact, mercurial and treacherous, he was always ready to change sides in search of the sensations he prized. One of very few war correspondents allowed on the Eastern Front in the summer of 1941 after the Germans had launched their invasion of the Soviet Union, he went because for him war was the supreme aesthetic experience. But it is not always possible to know what he witnessed and what he later imagined.

At times his reports seem wilfully fantastic. In *Kaputt* he recounts coming on a ice-covered lake in the depth of the Finnish wilderness, where hundreds of horses had died and been frozen: 'The lake looked like a vast sheet of white marble on which rested hundreds upon hundreds of horses' heads. They appeared to have been chopped off cleanly with an axe. Only the heads stuck out of the crust of ice. And they were all facing the shore. The white flame of terror still burnt in their wide-open eyes. Close to the shore a tangle of wildly rearing horses rose from the prison of ice.' Whether Malaparte ever saw anything at all resembling such a scene cannot be known. Were these scenes surreal versions of actual events? Or was he reporting hallucinations he had actually experienced? What is clear is that they are what he went to the front to see.

Much of the time Malaparte's dispatches from the front were realistic and accurate. In some cases they were also prescient. When he predicted that the war with the Soviet Union would be long and uncertain in its outcome, he was expelled by the Germans and placed under house arrest by Mussolini.

Malaparte claimed to enjoy living in the forests. This may not have been entirely true – he also claimed to be happiest when relaxing in luxurious hotels – but there was something genuine in his protestations, a feeling of self-loathing. In the forest, he wrote, humans became more authentically human:

> Nothing makes men so mutually hostile, nothing has a power to arouse them and to bring them into conflict, nothing renders them so callous and inexorable, as the preternatural violence of the forest. In the forest man rediscovers his primordial instincts. His most primitive animal impulses return to the surface, break through the delicate tracery of his nerves, reappear outside his veneer of civilized conventions and inhibitions in all their exquisite and squalid virginity.

If Malaparte liked life in the wilderness, it was because it helped him forget that he was a modern human being of the kind he despised. The ancient pagans did not imagine that humanity had been corrupted by civilization. They knew that what emerges when civilization breaks down is only barbarism, a disease of civilization. There are not two kinds of human being, savage and civilized. There is only the human animal, forever at war with itself.

After the war Malaparte swung to the left, claiming to see in Maoism a force for spiritual renewal, and when he died he was planning a visit to China. In his last days he was received into the Catholic Church, and around the same time accepted into the Italian communist party. Was he making a judicious retreat from pagan aestheticism as his vitality waned? Or was his double conversion proof of his paganism, a last-minute act of piety towards local cults? Whatever the answer, Malaparte seems to have died having reached an accommodation with himself.

INVISIBLE INK, FLAYED SKIN AND WHITE ANTS

Arthur Koestler's account of the career of the central protagonist of his novel *Darkness at Noon* (1940) has many parallels with Koestler's own life. A communist convicted on false charges of treason against the Soviet state he had helped bring into being, Rubashov had a mystical experience while in his cell awaiting execution in which the prospect of death no longer mattered. Captured and sentenced to death as a communist spy by Franco's forces in the Spanish Civil War, Koestler had a similar experience. Describing how his view of the world was changed, he wrote, 'In my youth I regarded the universe as an open book, printed in the language of physical equations and social determinants, whereas now it appears to me as a text written in invisible ink.'

What Koestler believed he had glimpsed was a text whose meaning could not be put into words. For the writer as for his fictional alter ego, the experience meant abandoning the certainty that only the material world is real. Rubashov is executed at the end of the novel. Exchanged for a prisoner held by Republican forces, Koestler was himself released and spent the rest of his life trying to understand what he had seen in the cell.

Published in 1954, Koestler called the memoir in which he recounted his mystical experience *The Invisible Writing*. The book testifies to Koestler's discovery that 'a higher order of reality existed, and that it alone invested existence with meaning'. Even as it evaporated, the experience left in its wake:

> a wordless essence, a fragrance of eternity, a quiver of the arrow in the blue . . . I must have stood there for some minutes, entranced, with a wordless awareness that 'this is perfect – perfect', until I noticed some slight mental discomfort nagging at the back of my mind – some trivial circumstance that marred the perfection of the moment. Then I remembered the nature of that irrelevant annoyance; I was, of course, in prison and might be shot. But this was immediately answered by a feeling whose verbal translation would be: 'So what? is that all? have you got nothing more serious to worry about?' – an answer so spontaneous, fresh and amused as if the impending annoyance had

been the loss of a collar-stud. Then I was floating on my back in a river of peace, under bridges of silence, it came from nowhere and flowed nowhere. Then there was no river and no 'I'. The 'I' had ceased to exist.

When in the early 1930s Koestler became an agent of the Soviet-controlled Comintern, an international communist front organization founded in Moscow in 1919, he did so partly from a need for intellectual order. He had seen the light – the light of reason – and a pattern had been revealed. Reading Lenin's *State and Revolution*, 'something had clicked in my brain which shook me like a mental explosion. To say that one has "seen the light" is a poor description of the mental rapture which only the convert knows ... The new light seems to pour across the skull; the whole universe falls into a pattern like the stray pieces of a large jigsaw assembled by magic at one stroke.'

The search for a pattern in events led him to Marxism-Leninism, which claimed to have discovered an unfolding logic in history. Having found the pattern, Koestler and his fellow communists felt obliged to be ruthlessly consistent in conforming to it.

Working for the Comintern Koestler travelled to the Ukraine during its man-made famine, when anything between four and eight million peasants (the numbers cannot be known with any precision) died as a result of the confiscation of grain for export. Witnessing mass starvation, he nonetheless used his journalism to debunk reports of food shortages: only a few rich peasants suffered in any serious way, he wrote. At times his ruthlessness was more personal. Travelling on behalf of the party in the Soviet Union he had an affair with an attractive young woman, a 'former person' from the old upper classes, whom he then reported to the secret police. Later he would feel remorse for betraying the woman, but at the time the fates of individuals seemed not to matter to him – even if the individual was himself.

Dedicating his life to a pattern in history, Rubashov ended as one of history's casualties. Koestler also dedicated a part of his life to a pattern in history, only to find one that was outside of time. He seems never to have accepted that chaos might be final. The world had to be rational, even if its logic could not be grasped by human reason.

Koestler was possessed by a search for total solutions, and it is easy to conclude that he would have done better to dedicate himself to piecemeal improvement. Yet this accusation, made by generations of comfortable liberals, shows a failure to understand the situation with which Koestler was contending. Liberal humanists believe that humanity advances to a better world in stages, slowly, in step-by-step increments: while an earthly paradise may be unachievable, incremental improvement is always possible. This philosophy – sometimes called meliorism – is presented as being at odds with any kind of utopianism. In interwar Europe, however, it was the idea of gradual progress that was truly utopian.

A sense that the world was descending into chaos shaped Koestler's generation. Born in 1905 into a prosperous, highly cultivated Jewish family, Koestler experienced the collapse of Europe's bourgeois civilization. He cast himself as the mortal enemy of the bourgeoisie – and, as a communist, so he was. At another level, he turned to communism in order to renew bourgeois life in a more durable form. Faced with the chaos of interwar Europe, he replaced the illusion of step-by-step advance by a myth of revolutionary transformation. It was not long before he realized that this too was an illusion.

In *Scum of the Earth* (1941), Koestler describes how after being released in Spain he returned to France. When war broke out he was interned in a camp and then released. He had a last meeting with the literary critic Walter Benjamin, who gave him half of his supply of morphine tablets to be taken in the event of capture by the Nazis. Benjamin fled to the French border with Spain, where he used the tablets to end his life. Seriously considering suicide on several occasions, and at one point swallowing some of Benjamin's tablets, Koestler eluded death partly by chance and partly through his own resourcefulness. Joining the Foreign Legion and then deserting, he escaped from France by way of North Africa and Lisbon, reaching Britain in November 1940.

A factual report of the disintegration of French society under German occupation, *Scum of the Earth* is also an exercise in self-examination. Observing at close quarters the fall of France, Koestler abandoned the beliefs that had guided his life until then. He had imagined that humankind longs for freedom. Now he came to think that humans were incurably irrational: 'Perhaps Hitler's genius was not demagogy, not lying, but the fundamentally irrational approach to the masses, the appeal to the pre-logical, totemistic mentality.'

Looking for a metaphor to capture the French collapse, Koestler turned to the world of insects. He writes that when he heard the news that Sedan, where French and British forces had been resisting the German advance, had been evacuated, he was reading the Belgian author Maurice Maeterlinck's *Life of the Termites* (1926), a study of the white ant. 'All this destruction', Maeterlinck had written,

is carried out without one's perceiving a living soul. For these insects, which are blind, are endowed with the genius to accomplish their task without being seen. The work is done under the cover of silence and only an alert ear is able to recognise the noise of the nibbling of millions of jaws in the night, which devour the framework of the building and prepare for its collapse . . . A planter enters his house after an absence of five or six days; everything is apparently as he left it, nothing is changed. He sits down on a chair, it collapses. He grabs the table to regain his balance, it falls to pieces under his hands. He leans against the central pillar, which gives way and brings down the roof in a cloud of dust.

Koestler's experience of the fall of France was similar to the planter's when entering the house. 'This was the moment when the chair under us broke down. What came after was just staggering and swaying about in a collapsing house, where everything you tried to hold onto turned into a handful of dust under your touch.'

Koestler grasped a fact liberal meliorists refuse to face: gradual progress is often impossible. When the illusion of piecemeal improvement was shattered by events, he – along with many in his generation – came to think that catastrophes were a necessary part of human advance. Famine and civil war, mass murder and brutal dictatorship were stages on the way to a world better than any that had previously existed.

As a working faith this had some advantages. The

savage conflicts of interwar Europe could be seen as a necessary stage from which order would emerge. As Koestler soon saw, the project in which this faith was embodied – the Soviet experiment – was just another disaster. Millions were flayed alive so that a new skin could be sewn on to their bleeding bodies. Many of the subjects of the experiment perished, while those who survived did so in their old, scarred human flesh. But when he worked for the Soviet cause, Koestler was not defaulting on some lofty liberal ideal of rational improvement. He was acting on the basis of an assessment of the European situation that was entirely realistic.

The ultimate disaster of a Nazi-ruled Europe was averted, but Koestler did not relapse into the liberal faith in gradual progress. Instead he turned away from politics. In later life he devoted himself to the study of paranormal psychology and unorthodox trends in biology, hoping they might give scientific substance to what he had seen in the prison cell. He failed to find what he was looking for. Suffering from leukaemia and Parkinson's disease, he committed suicide with his wife in 1983.

Koestler's excursions into mysticism and para-psychology are easily dismissed as fantasies. At best they can be described as interesting speculations. Yet they are not as fantastic as the idea that humanity is slowly ascending to a higher civilization.

THE EMPEROR'S TOMB

In his autobiography *The World of Yesterday* (1942), the writer Stefan Zweig described the Habsburg Empire in which he grew up as 'a world of security':

> Everything in our almost thousand-year-old Austrian monarchy seemed based on permanency, and the State itself was the chief guarantor of this stability . . . Our currency the Austrian crown, circulated in bright gold pieces, an assurance of its immutability. Everyone knew how much he possessed or what he was entitled to, what was permitted and what was forbidden . . . In this vast empire everything stood firmly and immovably in its appointed place, and at its head was the aged emperor; and were he to die, one knew (or believed) another would come to take his place, and nothing would change in the well-regulated order. No one thought of wars, of revolutions, or revolts. All that was radical, all violence, seemed impossible in an age of reason.

Zweig's view left out much that was rackety and uncertain in the far-flung Habsburg realm. Even so, the world he described did exist – until the First World War put an end to it. Throughout much of Europe rival armies of the dispossessed struggled for power in what soon became a fight to the death. With the assistance of Woodrow Wilson, the American prophet of national self-determination who set the seal on the destruction of the Habsburg order at the Versailles peace conference, Europe became a battlefield of ethnic groups. The middle classes were ruined as economic life swung from inflation to deflation and back to hyper-inflation, while workers suffered mass unemployment. Politics splintered into extremist fragments, with communist and fascist movements rejecting democracy and moderate parties powerless to hold the centre ground.

The old order had blown up, and there was nothing to replace it. Not only were the interests and objectives of social and ethnic groups in conflict. Ideals and values were irreconcilably opposed. In these circumstances gradual improvement was just another utopian dream. Progress in civilization seems possible only in interludes when history is idling.

In *The Emperor's Tomb*, a novella published in 1938, Joseph Roth captured one of the last of these interludes in his lifetime when he described a railway station in the summer of 1914:

The railway station was tiny . . . All little stations in all little provincial towns looked alike in the old Austro-Hungarian Empire. Small and painted yellow, they were like lazy cats lying in the snow in winter and in the summer, protected by the glass roof over the platform, and watched by the black double eagle on its yellow background. The porter was the same everywhere, in Sipolje as in Zlotogrod, his paunch stuffed into his inoffensive dark blue uniform, and across his chest the black belt into which was tucked his bell, whose prescribed treble peal announced the departure of a train. In Zlotogrod, too, as in Sipolje, there hung above the station-master's office, on the platform, the black iron contraption out of which, miraculously, sounded the distant silvery ringing of the telephone, delicate and enchanting signals from other worlds which made one wonder why they took refuge in such small but weighty lodging. On Zlotogrod station, as in Sipolje, the porter saluted the coming in of the train and its going out, and his salute was a kind of military blessing.

That world ended with the First World War and its aftermath. The trigger for the catastrophe was an assassination that could very easily not have occurred. The Serb nationalist Gavrilo Princip who shot dead Franz Ferdinand in Sarajevo on 28 June 1914 was part of a gang that had tried to blow up the Archduke just after ten o'clock that morning. The attempt failed, Franz Ferdinand laughed it off and the motorcade continued to his official engagement.

When the event was over he returned to his car, which left with others in the motorcade. But the driver took a wrong turning, the car came to a standstill and Princip, who had gone to a nearby delicatessen after the failed bomb attempt, was able to shoot the Archduke at close range. Had the driver not taken the turning he did, the engine not stalled or Princip not gone to the delicatessen, the assassination would not have taken place. Once it had, everything else followed.

Looking back on the Habsburg realm from the vantage-point of Europe in the 1930s, the vision Roth called up was richly embellished by memory. Yet it is true that the world whose loss he mourned lacked the worst human stains of the one that was to come. The Habsburg Empire was not a modern state, not even during the sixty-odd years when under the rule of its last emperor Franz Joseph it embraced the latest advances in modern technology, such as railways and the telegraph. In the ramshackle order of Franz Joseph, ancient evils, which more modern states revive in the pursuit of a better world, were in some degree tamed. Torture had been abolished by the empress Maria Theresa in 1776. Bigotry and hatred were not lacking – *fin de siècle* Vienna had a virulently anti-Semitic mayor, for example. Still, the absence of democracy in the Habsburg system served as a barrier against the xenophobic mass movements that would later sweep across central Europe. The inhabitants of the empire were subjects rather than citizens – a status that deprived them of the pleasure of justifying hatred by reference to ideals of self-government. Only with the struggle for national self-determination did it come to be believed that every human being had to belong to a group defined in opposition to others.

Roth analysed this process in a short story, 'The Bust of the Emperor' (1935). Some years before the Great War, he writes,

> the so-called 'nationality question' began to be acute in the monarchy. Everyone aligned them-selves – whether they wanted to, or merely pre-tended to want to – with one or other of the many peoples there used to be in the old monarchy. For it had been discovered in the course of the nine-teenth century that every individual has to belong to a particular race or nation, if he wanted to be a fully rounded bourgeois individual . . . all those people who had never been other than Austrians, in Tarnopol, in Sarajevo, in Vienna, in Brunn, in Prague, in Czernowitz, in Oderburg, in Troppau, never anything other than Austrians: they now began, in compliance with the 'order of the day', to call themselves part of the Polish, the Czech, the Ukrainian, the German, the Romanian, the

Slovenian, the Croatian 'nation' – and so on and. so forth.

With the break-up of the Habsburg monarchy, these newly formed groups were able to take their place in the struggle for land and power that followed. As Roth had foreseen, the archaic devices of empire were replaced by modern emblems of blood and soil.

Starting as a progressive who looked eagerly to the future, Roth ended as a reactionary who looked back fondly on the empire of Franz Joseph. He knew his nostalgia was futile. The old monarchy had been destroyed not only by the Great War but by the power of modern ideals. How could any believer in progress accept a type of authority that rested on the accidents of history? Yet the struggle for power that ensued once the antique order of empire had gone was barbaric and pitiless.

Along with the formation of nations there was the 'problem of national minorities'. Ethnic cleansing – the forcible expulsion and migration of these minorities – was an integral part of building democracy in central and eastern Europe. Progressive thinkers viewed this process as a stage on the way to universal self-determination. Roth had no such illusions. He knew the end-result could only be mass murder. Writing to Zweig in 1933, he warned: 'We are drifting towards great catastrophes . . . it all leads to a new war. I won't bet a penny on our lives. They have established a reign of barbarity.'

Roth escaped the fate he foresaw for himself and others. He fled Germany, where he had written for the liberal *Frankfurter Zeitung*, to settle in Paris where he produced some of his finest novels, short stories and journalism. He died there of alcoholic cirrhosis in 1939. When he was buried a representative of the Habsburg monarchy and a delegate from the communist party stood side by side at the grave, where Jewish and Catholic prayers were said. Zweig survived longer, leaving Austria in 1934, living in Britain and the US, then moving to Brazil in 1941. A year later, fearing an Axis victory after the fall of Singapore, he committed suicide together with his wife, only days after finishing *The World of Yesterday* and posting the manuscript to the publisher.

TWO TIMES TWO EQUALS FIVE

When Winston Smith is being tortured in George Orwell's *1984*, the interrogator O'Brien holds up four fingers and demands that Smith tell him truthfully that there are five. O'Brien will not be satisfied with a lie extorted under pressure. He wants Smith to *see* five fingers. The interrogation is lengthy and agonizing:

'You are a slow learner, Winston,' said O'Brien gently.

'How can I help it?' he blubbered. 'How can I help seeing what is in front of my eyes? Two and two are four.'

'Sometimes, Winston. Sometimes they are five. Sometimes they are three. Sometimes they are all of them at the same time. You must try harder. It is not easy to become sane.'

Smith is subjected to further torture – but not as a punishment, O'Brien explains. In past times inquisitors had forced those they tortured to confess; but the confessions were not believed, either by those who made them or by others. In time the tortured came to be revered as martyrs and the torturers reviled as tyrants. O'Brien tells Winston of the progress that has been achieved since those days:

We do not make mistakes of that kind. All the confessions that are uttered here are true. We make them true. And above all we do not allow the dead to rise up against us. You must stop imagining that posterity will vindicate you, Winston. Posterity will never hear of you. You will be lifted clean out of the stream of history. We shall turn you into gas and pour you into the stratosphere. Nothing will remain of you; not your name in a register, not a memory in a living brain. You will be annihilated in the past as well as the future. You will never have existed.

Smith must come to see five fingers whenever he is told to do so; but he must do so freely: 'O'Brien smiled slightly. "You are a flaw in the pattern, Winston. You are a stain that must be wiped out. Did I not tell you that we are different from the persecutors of the past? We are not content with negative obedience, nor even with the most abject submission. When finally you surrender to us, it must be of your own free will."' Winston had written in his diary, 'Freedom is the freedom to say that two and two make four.' O'Brien aims to make Winston accept that two and two make five. Once Winston sees that to be true, he will be saved.

The idea that freedom is the ability to say two and two make four appeared in Orwell's writings before he published *1984*. The novel appeared in 1949, but in his essay 'Looking Back on the Spanish War', written in 1942, Orwell noted:

Nazi theory specifically denies that such a thing as 'the truth' exists. There is, for instance, no such thing as 'science'. There is only 'German science', 'Jewish science' etc. The implied objective of this line of thought is a world in which the Leader, or

some ruling cliqu... ...uture
but *the past*. If the Lea... ...such an
event, 'It never happened' ...ever happened. If he says that two and two are five – well,
two and two are five.

It has been suggested that Orwell derived the
phrase from the Nazi Hermann Göring, who is
reported to have declared, 'If the Führer wants it, two
and two make five.' But another source exists in a
book Orwell reviewed in the *New English Weekly* in
June 1938. In Chapter Fifteen of Book Two of his
book *Assignment in Utopia*, which is entitled 'Two
Plus Two Equals Five', Eugene Lyons wrote of his
time in the Soviet Union in the 1930s:

Industrialization went forward with a great roar
and frenzied war whoops. Reports of building,
factory output, new collectives and state farms
elbowed all other news off the front pages. There
was constant beating of alarm drums: a breach on
one or another economic front, cries of sabotage,
sudden arrests and shooting of engineers and
administrators. Notwithstanding, plans were everywhere fulfilled and even surpassed. New energies
and enthusiasms, new threats as well, were having
their effect . . .
   Optimism ran amuck. Every new statistical

success gave another justification for the coercive policies by which it was achieved. Every setback · was another stimulus to the same policies. The slogan 'The Five Year Plan in Four Years' was advanced, and the magic symbols '5-in-4' and '2 + 2 = 5' were posted and shouted throughout the land.

The formula 2 + 2 = 5 instantly riveted my attention. It seemed to me at once bold and pre-posterous – the daring and the paradox and the tragic absurdity of the Soviet scene, its mystical simplicity, its defiance of logic, all reduced to nose-thumbing arithmetic . . . 2 + 2 = 5: in elec-tric lights on Moscow housefronts, in foot-high letters on billboards, spelled planned error, hyper-bole, perverse optimism; something childishly headstrong and strikingly imaginative . . .

A sense of reality given him by his hard early life may account for Lyons's inability to accept the magi-cal arithmetic of the Five Year Plan. Born in 1898 in Belarus, then part of the Russian empire, he grew up in a poor district of New York City. After serving in the US army in the First World War he became involved in radical activity, defending the anarchists Sacco and Vanzetti, who were executed for taking part in an armed robbery but of whose innocence Lyons was convinced, and becoming a fellow-traveller of the

American communist party. Drifting into journalism, he started working for the *Daily Worker*. In the years 1923–7 he worked for the Soviet news agency TASS and in 1928–34 for the American United Press agency (UPI) as their man in Moscow, where he was invited to a personal interview with Stalin.

Arriving a firm believer in the Soviet system, he took part in a concerted campaign inspired by Soviet censors to discredit the Welsh journalist Gareth Jones, a former private secretary to the British prime minister Lloyd George, whose reports on the famine in Ukraine were a source of embarrassment to the Soviet authorities. From the account he gives in *Assignment in Utopia*, 'The Press Corps Conceals a Famine', it seems that Lyons's reasons for taking part in the campaign were partly pragmatic. Like the rest of the correspondents, he feared his visa would be withdrawn if he did not co-operate with the Soviet censor. If that happened he would lose his usefulness to his newspaper and find himself unemployed in the depths of the Depression. Lyons and the rest of the press corps published a series of articles attacking Jones and remained as working correspondents. Jones was expelled from the Soviet Union and carried on his work in the Far East, where he was killed in a bandit attack in 1935 that some have suggested might have been instigated by the Soviet security services.

By the time he took part in the campaign to

discredit Jones, Lyons saw the realities of Soviet life as clearly as the campaigning Welsh journalist did. Very few of the books written by westerners who travelled in the Soviet Union include any mention of sights that were commonplace at the time: the feral children who haunted railway stations, survivors from the millions of orphans created by the Civil War, waifs who disappeared as they were seized and disposed of by the security organs, then swelled again in numbers when another generation of orphans was created as part of the collectivization of farming; the peasants themselves being herded on to trains 'at provincial railroad points, under G.P.U. guards, like bewildered animals, staring vacantly into space. These meek, bedraggled, work-worn creatures were scarcely the kulaks [rich capitalist peasants] of the propaganda posters. The spectacle of peasants being led by soldiers with drawn revolvers through the streets even of Moscow was too commonplace to win more than a casual glance from the crowds on the sidewalks.'

It was not only the deportation of peasants at gunpoint that escaped the attention of western visitors. Very few mentioned the special shops where people with access to 'valuta' could buy goods inaccessible to ordinary Russians. When used in connection with these shops, valuta meant foreign currency or credit slips acquired by selling gold – the only means whereby the goods could be bought, though the prices were quoted in rubles. As Lyons reports, valuta had a more general meaning – 'real values' – which was applied in many contexts: 'Valuta shops, valuta restaurants, valuta arrests, valuta tortures, valuta whores: just a few dimensions of that inexhaustible word.'

Lyons describes the luxuries in one such store in Moscow:

> The miracle of white bread: crisp little loaves in a glowing heap on the . . . counter. Not the sand-gray bread that passed, at ruble prices, for white in the ruble stores, but luminously real. At the other end of the shop was the jewelry department. Its glitter of rubies and diamonds for foreign buyers had not half the radiance of the white loaves; precious stones shine with a cold inner glitter, whereas white loaves are prisms to reflect fascination in the eyes of hungry Russians. There was butter, too, and cheeses, bland Volga salmon and great flanks of blood-dripping meat. But the white bread outshone them all – at once substance and symbol of desire.

Russians who had gold – 'tsarist coins, spoons, trinkets, wedding rings, old dental plates' – took it to a counter in the shop where they received a credit slip in return. Later, special coupons were issued to facilitate the process, so that the slips became a currency of their own, thirty to sixty times as valuable as the Soviet ruble.

For Russians using the stores was not without risk, but hunger and despair left them with no other option. Though the authorities had announced that no identity checks would be made, the secret police made thousands of arrests based on information passed on from the shops. Anyone suspected of possessing gold or other valuables was routinely tortured, though most of those who had precious items had acquired them legally. Torture techniques included the 'sweat room', the 'lice room', the 'conveyor', 'cold treatments' and other methods. If those suspected failed to reveal a hoard of precious goods, their children would be tortured – a process that could be quite lengthy if the victims did not have any precious items. Those tortured were often Jews, who were believed to have valuta because they sometimes received money from relatives in America.

Though the practice of valuta torture was known to many western correspondents, none mentioned it in their dispatches. To do so would have been an act of defiance that would have ended their careers. What is more curious is that so very few western visitors noticed the hungry, frightened state of ordinary Russians.

One of the reasons for valuta torture was a decline in income from Soviet exports. The Soviet Union in the 1930s was as badly hit by the Depression as western countries. Yet dignitaries who had very little to lose by speaking their minds – Bernard Shaw and Lady Astor, among others – were able to visit the country and return with glowing reports of social improvement. In returning to America a confirmed anti-communist Lyons belonged in a tiny minority. For the most part, western pilgrims to the Soviet Union happily accepted the pseudo-reality they were shown. Possessed by a vision of progress, they had no difficulty in accepting that two times two can make five.

O'Brien had told Winston that reality was a human construction:

You believe that reality is something objective, external, existing in its own right . . . When you delude yourself into thinking that you see something, you assume that everyone sees the same thing you do. But I tell you, Winston, that reality is not external. Reality exists in the human mind, and nowhere else. Not in the individual mind, which can make mistakes, and in any case soon perishes: only in the mind of the party, which is collective and immortal. Whatever the party holds to be truth, *is* truth.

O'Brien does not say the party flouts the laws of arithmetic. He says the laws of arithmetic are whatever the party wants them to be. Remaking the world in any way it liked, the party would be in power for ever. 'The party seeks power for its own sake,' he tells Winston. 'We are not interested in the good of others; we are interested solely in power. Not wealth or luxury or long life or happiness: only power, pure power.' This power is above all over human beings; but it is also power over the material world. 'Already our control over matter is absolute . . . There is nothing that we could not do. Invisibility, levitation – anything . . . You must get rid of those nineteenth-century ideas about the laws of Nature. We make the laws of Nature.' In the world that O'Brien is making, there is only power: 'If you want a picture of the future, imagine a boot stamping on a human face – forever.'

In a curious inversion, Orwell's interpretation of 'two and two make five' is the opposite of that of Dostoevsky, in whose writings the laws of arithmetic are first used to mount a critique of utopianism. In 1984, it is the formula 'two plus two makes five' that nullifies human freedom. In *Notes from Underground*, it is 'two times two equals four' that is rejected as a fetter on freedom. The underground man rebels against the 'crystal palace' of rationalism. By discovering and obeying the laws of nature, progressive thinkers believed, humanity could create a world without tyranny. But, for the underground man, it is these universal laws – 'stone walls' as he calls them – that block the way to freedom: 'Good Lord, what do I care about the laws of nature and arithmetic when for some reason I dislike all these laws and I dislike the fact that two times two makes four? Of course, I won't break through that wall with my head if I don't really have the strength to do so, nor will I reconcile myself to it just because I'm faced with such a stone wall and lack the strength.' Aiming to realize human freedom by obeying universal laws, the crystal palace would destroy the ability to act in defiance of these laws – the most fundamental freedom of all.

The project against which Winston revolts is the opposite of that against which Dostoevsky's underground man rebels. Instead of preaching submission to universal laws as did nineteenth-century rationalists, O'Brien claims the power to make these laws. Yet the two projects serve the same infantile fantasy: the magical omnipotence of thought. Whether affirmed in the terms of classical logic or denied in those of romantic will, the message is the same: the human mind is the measure of reality. In the twentieth century, the two projects merged to a point where they could hardly be told apart. Asserting that humankind progresses by overcoming contradictions, the dialectical logic of Marxism-Leninism spawned the arithmetical magic that Lyons observed in action.

Contrary to generations of western progressives, it was not Russian backwardness or mistakes in applying Marxian theory that produced the society that Lyons observed. Similar regimes came into being wherever the communist project was attempted. Lenin's Russia, Mao's China, Ceausescu's Romania and many more were variants of a single dictatorial model. From being a movement aiming for universal freedom, communism turned into a system of universal despotism. That is the logic of utopia. If *1984* is such a powerful myth, one reason is that it captures this truth.

Yet there is a flaw in Orwell's story, which emerges in his picture of the all-powerful interrogator. The dystopia of perpetual power is a fantasy, and so is O'Brien. Soviet torturers were sweating functionaries living in constant fear. Like their victims, they knew that they were resources that would be used up in the service of power. There was no inner-party elite safe from the contingencies of history.

Reality was not constructed in the former Soviet Union, only for a while denied. Beneath the slogans was an actually existing world in which the soil and lakes were poisoned from over-rapid industrialization, vast and useless projects were built at enormous human cost and everyday life was a predatory struggle for survival. Millions died needlessly and tens of millions suffered broken lives, most leaving barely a trace they had ever existed. But under the surface powerful currents were flowing, which in time would wash away the pseudo-reality that enchanted western pilgrims. The Soviet dystopia ended by becoming just another piece of rubbish in the debris of history.

WHAT A TYRANT
CAN DO FOR YOU

The German liberal journalist Sebastian Haffner, who observed Hitler's rise until he was forced to flee to London with his Jewish fiancée in 1938, believed that, among those it did not terrorize or murder, Nazi Germany had succeeded in creating a condition of collective happiness. Writing in 1979 he noted:

> Where the lives of the vast majority of Germans, who were not racially or politically rejected or per-secuted, differed in the Third Reich from their life in pre-Hitler Germany, and also from that in the pre-sent Federal Republic, and where they resembled present life in the GDR [German Democratic Republic] like two peas in a pod, was that by far the greater portion of them took part in extra-domestic

communities or 'collectives' which the majority, whether membership was officially compulsory or not, were unable in practice to avoid . . . Of course the songs that were sung and the speeches that were made were different in the Third Reich from those in the GDR today. But the activities, rambling, marching and camping, singing and celebrating, model making, PT and firearms drill, were indistinguishable, just as much as the undeniable sense of security, comradeship and happiness which flourished in such communities. In that he forced the people into this happiness Hitler undoubtedly was a socialist – indeed a very effective socialist.

Was it happiness? Or did the compulsion make people feel unhappy? In the GDR at present people often try to escape from their enforced happiness; but when they get to the Federal Republic they just as often complain about their loneliness, which is the other side of the coin of individual liberty. Things were probably similar in the Third Reich. We shall not try here to decide the question who is happier, socialized man or man living as an individual.

Haffner answered his own question in *Defying Hitler*, a memoir of his life in Germany that he began in 1939, shortly after he arrived in Britain as an exile from Germany. The book was published only in 2002 at the instigation of Haffner's son, three years after his father's death at the age of ninety-one.

Many Germans were happy under Nazism: 'It is said that the Germans are subjugated. That is only half true. They are also something else, something worse, for which there is no word: they are "comraded", a dreadfully dangerous condition. They live a drugged life in a dream world. They are terribly happy, but terribly demeaned; so self-satisfied, but so boundlessly loathsome; so proud and yet so despicable and inhuman. They think they are scaling high mountains, when in reality they are crawling in a swamp.'

The happiness Haffner witnessed in Nazi Germany coexisted with terror. But, for many Germans, terror and happiness were not at odds. Haffner writes:

European history knows two forms of terror. The first is the uncontrollable explosion of bloodlust in a mass uprising. The other is cold, calculated cruelty committed by a victorious state as a demonstration of power and intimidation. The two forms of terror normally correspond to revolution and repression. The first is revolutionary. It justifies itself by the rage and fever of the moment, a temporary madness. The second is repressive. It justifies itself by the preceding revolutionary atrocities.

It was left to the Nazis to combine both forms of

terror in a manner that invalidates both justifications.

Joining the two types of terror into a single system, the Nazis used it to create the comradeship that Haffner describes.

The collective solidarity of Nazi Germany was sustained by the incessant creation of internal enemies. Gays, gypsies and Jews were not only discriminated against as they had been in the past. They were actively persecuted, and this was essential to the collective euphoria that was created by the Nazi regime.

As the writer Victor Klemperer records in his diaries, where he describes the persecution to which he and his non-Jewish wife were subject in the Nazi years – which included being forced to have their cat put down when pets were forbidden to Jews – there were times when they were shown kindness by neighbours and shopkeepers, who slipped them food and chocolate bars. Fortunately, popular solidarity is never total. Yet there can be no doubt that the suffering inflicted on Jews was an integral part of the happiness the Nazis succeeded in manufacturing in the rest of the population. In order to make it appetizing, the thin gruel of communal joy had to be richly spiced with cruelty.

Though they used the ballot box when it suited

them, the Nazis were an insurrectionary movement. Hitler came to power by overthrowing the Weimar republic, a liberal regime; democracy was undermined and replaced by tyranny. *Bien-pensants* will insist that revolt against tyranny has a different dynamic, and it is true that revolutionaries may be genuine lovers of liberty. But, in the course of the revolutions for which they fight, most are erased from history.

By toppling the tyrant people are free to tyrannize over one another. A period of anarchy often intervenes, which rarely lasts for long. A need for order soon prevails. But the coldly repressive terror that accompanies the consolidation of a new regime may not be as different from revolutionary bloodlust as Haffner maintains. Both amount to a collective psychosis, a response that has been used throughout history to adapt to extreme conditions. Tyranny offers relief from the burden of sanity and a licence to enact forbidden impulses of hatred and violence. By acting on these impulses and releasing them in their subjects tyrants give people a kind of happiness, which as individuals they may be incapable of achieving.

The overthrow of the *ancien régime* in France, the Tsars in Russia, the Shah of Iran, Saddam in Iraq and Mubarak in Egypt may have produced benefits for many people, but increased freedom was not among them. Mass killing, attacks on minorities, torture on a larger scale, another kind of tyranny, often more cruel than the one that was overthrown – these have been the results. To think of humans as freedom-loving, you must be ready to view nearly all of history as a mistake.

ICHTHYOPHILS AND LIBERALS

In *From the Other Shore*, a collection of essays and dialogues written by Alexander Herzen between 1847 and 1851, the radical Russian journalist imagines a dialogue between a believer in human freedom and a sceptic who judges humans by their behaviour rather than by their professed ideals. To the surprise of the believer, the sceptic quotes Rousseau's dictum, 'Man is born to be free – and is everywhere in chains!' But the sceptic does so only in order to mock Rousseau's rousing declaration: 'I see in it a violation of history and contempt for facts. I find that intolerable. Such caprice offends me. Besides, it is a dangerous procedure to state, a priori, as a fact, what is really the crux of the problem. What would you say to a man who, nodding his head sadly, remarked that "Fish are born to fly – but everywhere they swim!"?'

The sceptic goes on to present the argument of the

'ichthyophil', who believes that human beings long to be free:

> First of all he will point out to you that the skeleton of a fish clearly shows a tendency to develop the extremities into legs and wings. He will then show you perfectly useless little bones that are a hint of the bone of a leg or a wing. Then he will refer to flying fish, which prove, in fact, that *fishkind* not only aspires to fly, but also can do so on occasion. Having said all this in reply, he will be justified in asking you, in his turn, why you do not demand from Rousseau a justification for his statement that man must be free, seeing that he is always in chains. Why does everything else exist as it ought to exist, whereas with man, it is the opposite?

The question of the sceptic – a stand-in for Herzen himself – has yet to be answered. Writing in his memoir *My Past and Thoughts*, published in eight parts in the 1850s when he was living in exile, Herzen described how the pursuit of illusions – in modern times, the illusion of 'humanity' – has shaped the course of history:

> History has developed by means of absurdities; people have constantly set their hearts on chimeras,

and have achieved very real results. In waking dreams they have gone after the rainbow, sought now paradise in heaven, now heaven on earth, and on their way have sung everlasting songs, have decorated temples with their everlasting sculptures, have built Rome and Athens, Paris and London. One dream yields to another; the sleep *sometimes* becomes lighter, but is never quite gone. People will accept anything, believe in anything, submit to anything and are ready to sacrifice much; but they recoil in horror when through the gaping chink between two religions, which lets in the light of day, there blows upon them the cool wind of reason . . .

This is only to reaffirm the sceptic's diagnosis. Ichthyophils are devoted to their species as they believe it ought to be, not as it actually is or as it truly wants to be. Ichthyophils come in many varieties – the Jacobin, Bolshevik and Maoist, terrorizing humankind in order to remake it on a new model; the neo-conservative, waging perpetual war as a means to universal democracy; liberal crusaders for human rights, who are convinced that all the world longs to become as they imagine themselves to be.

Perhaps the most remarkable ichthyophils are the Romantics, who believe human individuality is everywhere repressed. Among them none is so well known as the author of *On Liberty* (1859), a seminal statement of ichthyophil philosophy. As Herzen summarized this view, John Stuart Mill was:

> horrified by the constant deterioration of personalities, taste and style, by the inanity of men's interests and their absence of vigour; he looks clearly, and sees clearly that everything is becoming shallow, commonplace, shoddy, trite, more 'respectable', perhaps, but more banal . . . he says to his contemporaries: 'Stop! Think again! Do you know where you are going? Look: *your soul is ebbing away.*'

> But why does he try to wake the sleepers? What path, what way out, has he devised for them? . . . Modern Europeans, he says, live in vain unrest, in senseless changes: 'In getting rid of singularities we do not get rid of changes, so long as they are performed each time by *everyone*. We have cast away our fathers' individual, personal way of dressing, and are ready to change the cut of our clothes two or three times a year, but only so long as everybody changes it; and this is done not with an eye to beauty or convenience but for the sake of change itself!' . . . So we have come back and are facing the same question. On what principle are we to wake the sleeper? In the name of what shall the

flabby personality, magnetised by trifles, be inspired to be discontented with its present life of railways, telegraphs, newspapers and cheap goods?

Ichthyophils imagine that human beings want a life in which they can make their own choices. But what if they can be fulfilled only by a life in which they follow each other? The majority who obey the fashion of the day may be acting on a secret awareness that they lack the potential for a truly individual existence.

Liberalism – the ichthyophil variety, at any rate – teaches that everyone yearns to be free. Herzen's experience of the abortive European revolutions of 1848 led him to doubt that this was so. It was because of his disillusionment that he criticized Mill so sharply. But if it is true that Mill was deluded in thinking that everyone loves freedom, it may also be true that without this illusion there would be still less freedom in the world. The charm of a liberal way of life is that it enables most people to renounce their freedom unknowingly. Allowing the majority of humankind to imagine they are flying fish even as they pass their lives under the waves, liberal civilization rests on a dream.

PAPER CLOTHES, GRAND PIANOS AND A MILLIARD BLADES OF GRASS

'Just before the First World War in 1913, the German mark, the British shilling, the French franc, and the Italian lira were all worth about the same, and four or five of any were worth about a dollar. At the end of 1923, it would have been possible to exchange a shilling, a franc or a lira for up to 1,000,000,000,000 marks, though in practice by then no one was willing to take marks in return for anything. The mark was dead, one million-millionth of its former self. It had taken ten years to die.'

As described by the historian Adam Fergusson in his book *When Money Dies: The Nightmare of the Weimar Hyper-Inflation* (1975, 2010), the death of money was a change in human experience that produced an infectious madness. The shock is captured in the account Fergusson cites of a middle-aged widow, who went to the bank to be told her life savings had lost three-quarters of their value. Remonstrating with the banker, she objected: 'Yes, but mine are government securities. Surely there can't be anything safer than that.' The banker replied: 'Where is the State which guaranteed these securities to you? It is dead.'

The widow goes to write in her diary that food

cost a hundred or two hundred times what it did in 1913. Though suits had not gone up as much in price, clothes made of paper were being sold instead. Drawing on a supply of her husband's cigars, the widow was able to barter for food. Others subsisted by selling what they had – a single link a day from a gold crucifix chain, a lump of coal for a shirt, a shirt for a bag of potatoes. Not all were so fortunate. The widow describes how 'every day, again and again, elderly, retired officials of high rank collapse on the streets of Vienna from hunger.' Most of them had simply fainted. 'In practice, people didn't just die.' Rather, they sold off the props of bourgeois life, one by one – a painting, a carpet, china, silver spoons – until they had nothing left. Even then, they managed to struggle on.

As in Naples, most people survived to suffer the destruction of the image they had formed of themselves as moral beings. Following the code of former times led only to ruin. With the peasants refusing to exchange food for worthless paper money, looting was the only recourse. The widow's daughter wrote describing how, while going to church at Linz, she came across 'all kinds of odd-looking individuals'. One man wore three hats, one on top of another, others were pulling along carts piled high with tins of food, yet others were changing from rags into new clothes. When the daughter reached Linz it 'looked as if it had been visited by an earthquake'. Shops had been ransacked and destroyed, horses and carts stolen and taken away, pigs killed or injured and left to die, cows slaughtered and meat torn from their bones. With money having no value, people consumed whatever they could find.

A feature of the time was a pervasive sense of unreality. Inconceivable numbers invaded everyone's life. Walter Rathenau, the German-Jewish industrialist who as foreign minister had the responsibility of handling the demands for reparations made by the Allies against Germany after the end of the First World War, wrote of statesmen and financiers, sitting in their offices, where they 'write down noughts, and nine noughts mean a milliard. A milliard comes easily and trippingly to the tongue, but no one can imagine a milliard. What is a milliard? Does a wood contain a milliard leaves? Are there a milliard blades of grass in a meadow? Who knows?' Rathenau was a victim of the delirium he had diagnosed. Returning home by car one evening in June 1922, he was ambushed, shot by assassins at close range and then blown up by a bomb.

In the terminology of the time a milliard meant one thousand million, a billion was a million millions and a billiard a thousand billion. By October 1923, the British ambassador noted, sums of less than a million marks were no longer dealt with and even beggars would not accept a smaller note. By 21 October, there were eight milliard marks to the pound. On the 26th the central bank was surrounded by a mob demanding milliard-mark notes. By 1 November, five-billiard and ten-billiard notes were ready for circulation.

In the flight from these unthinkable sums speculation became a mass frenzy. Any kind of tangible wealth was keenly sought after. Grand pianos became prized possessions among people who could not read a note of music. Yet very few of those caught up in the frenzy succeeded in protecting their wealth. An almost incalculable quantity of money was created, but nearly everyone was impoverished. Many of the pianos probably ended up being used as firewood.

THE ALCHEMISTS OF FINANCE

Around the end of the last century a new type of political economy was installed. In the past capitalism had recognized the danger of debt. Banks were limited in how much they could lend, so that the economy would not be based on too much borrowing. In the new capitalism it was believed that debt could create wealth: lend enough money to enough people, and soon all would be rich.

Real wealth is physical and intrinsically finite; made from things that are used up or rust away, it is eaten by time. Debt is potentially limitless, feeding on itself and increasing until it can never be paid off. The immaterial wealth created by the new capitalism was also potentially limitless. The practice of offering sub-prime mortgages, loans that could never be paid off from the income of the borrowers, has been described as predatory lending. So from one point of view it was. Unless house prices continued to rise, the borrowers were bound to default. The only clear beneficiaries were the banks which received commission for selling loans they knew could not be repaid.

From another point of view, the practice was a kind of alchemy. Lending people money they could not afford to borrow was a way of creating wealth out of nothing. Even as industry was being offshored and workers deskilled, prosperity would continue rising. Wealth need not be wrenched from the earth as in earlier times. Through a process whose workings no one could specify, wealth could be conjured into being. Among the alchemists of former times, the attempt to turn base metal into gold was known to be a type of magic – an attempt to bypass natural laws. Twenty-first-century practitioners of the putative discipline of economics lacked this insight. With few exceptions, they were left gawping when the alchemical experiment ended in farce and ruin.

The debt-based hyper-capitalism that sprang up in America in the closing decades of the twentieth century was always going to be short lived. House-holds with static or declining incomes cannot pay off spiralling debts. When the financial crisis erupted in 2007, the incomes of most Americans had been stagnant for over thirty years. Concealed by the credit boom, the majority were becoming poorer. A new American political economy was emerging: one in which a larger proportion of the population is incarcerated than in any other country, many are permanently unemployed, much of the workforce is casualized and large numbers subsist in a shadow-economy of drug dealing and sex work – a post-modern plantation economy where servitude can be found on every street corner.

According to some historians, inequality in America at the start of the twenty-first century is greater than in the slave-based economy of imperial Rome in the second century. Of course there are differences. Contemporary America is probably less stable than imperial Rome. It is hard to see how the volatile paper wealth of a few can be sustained on the basis of a decimated workforce in a hollowed-out economy. The insuperable problem of American capitalism may well turn out to be the declining profits of debt slavery.

It is not only mass poverty that makes the new capitalism hard to live in. In America more than any-where else the belief that each person's life can be a story of continuing improvement has been a part of the psyche. In the new economy, where a disjointed existence is the common lot, this is a story that makes no sense. When the meaning of life is projected into the future, how are people to live when the future can no longer be imagined? The rise of the Tea Party suggests a retreat into a kind of willed psychosis, with populist demagogues promising a return to a mythical past.

Something not altogether different is under way in Europe. While the working classes are becoming workless, the middle classes are turning into a new kind of proletariat. The end-result of the boom has been the erosion of savings and the destruction of professions. Austerity in Greece has resulted in a flight from the city to the countryside and reversion to a barter economy – a reverse form of economic development. In an irony that is somehow predictable, the determination to impose modernization is forcing a return to more primitive forms of life.

As the crash has continued, the passivity that accompanied its earlier stages has given way to resistance. Here too, though, many people dream of resuming the advance that seemed unstoppable a few years ago. The boom years were marked by faith in unending economic expansion, and now that the boom is over the demand for a return to growth is ubiquitous and insistent. The fact that real wealth is finite has not been accepted. The most likely scenario must be that a resumption of growth is engineered, only to be derailed at some point in the future by scarcities of oil, water and other natural resources.

The early twenty-first century has been compared with the 1930s, and there are similarities. Both feature a global dislocation and involve geopolitical shifts – in the interwar years from Europe to the US, today from east to west. In both cases it could be known in advance that Europe would descend into internecine conflict. There are now no mass movements – fascist, Nazi or communist – of the kind that ravaged interwar Europe. Democracy is unlikely to be replaced in any European country by the kind of dictatorship that came to power nearly everywhere on the European continent in the 1930s. But the forces of xenophobia are again on the march. Exacerbated by the determination of European elites to maintain a dysfunctional single currency, economic dislocation is producing a twenty-first-century version of the toxic politics of the interwar period. As in the 1930s, so today, minorities – immigrants, gypsies, gays, Jews – are being targeted as scapegoats.

The crisis today resembles that in the 1930s in a more basic respect: it cannot be overcome by collective action. It is part of the faith in progress that no human problem is in the long run insoluble. Marx declared in *A Contribution to the Critique of Political Economy* (1859) that 'humanity sets itself only such tasks as it is able to solve.' Right in thinking that capitalism contains a potential for self-destruction, Marx was wrong in believing that capitalism would be followed by a more lasting mode of production. Wealth can be created in many kinds of economic system, but never for long. The human animal consumes what it has produced, and then moves on.

The rise and fall of economic systems is the normal course of history. Today, while one kind of capitalism is declining, others – in China and India, Russia, Brazil and Africa – are advancing. Capitalism is not ending. It is changing its shape, as it has done many times before. How old and new capitalisms settle their conflicting claims over the Earth's resources in a time of rising human numbers remains to be seen.

The most serious problems are not resolved. More than anything enacted by Roosevelt, it was mass mobilization in the Second World War that lifted America, and eventually the world, out of the Great Depression. In the same way, the problems facing the world today will not be overcome by any kind of decision. Instead there will be a shift of scene, an alteration in the global landscape that no one can foresee or control, as a result of which difficulties that are presently intractable will be left behind.

HUMANISM AND FLYING SAUCERS

If belief in human rationality was a scientific theory it would long since have been abandoned. A striking falsification can be found in a classic of social psychology, *When Prophecy Fails* (1956), a study of a UFO cult in the early 1950s. Written by a team led by Leon Festinger, the psychologist who developed the idea of cognitive dissonance, the book recounts how a Michigan woman claimed to have received messages in automatic writing from alien intelligences on another planet announcing the end of the world, which would be inundated by a great flood in the hours before dawn on 21 December 1954. The woman and her disciples had left their homes, jobs and partners and given away their possessions, in order to be ready for the arrival of a flying saucer that would rescue them from the doomed planet.

For Festinger and his colleagues, this was an opportunity to test the theory of cognitive dissonance. According to the theory, human beings do not deal with conflicting beliefs and perceptions by testing them against facts. They reduce the conflict by reinterpreting facts that challenge the beliefs to which they are most attached. As T. S. Eliot wrote in *Burnt Norton*, humankind cannot bear very much reality.

In order to test the theory, the psychologists infiltrated themselves into the cult and observed the reaction when the apocalypse failed to occur. Just as the theory predicted, the cultists refused to accept that their system of beliefs was mistaken. Instead, they interpreted the failure of doomsday to arrive as evidence that by waiting and praying throughout the night they had succeeded in preventing it. The confounding of all their expectations only led them to cling more tightly to their faith, and they went on to proselytize for their beliefs all the more fervently.

As Festinger writes, summarizing this process:

> Suppose an individual believes something with his whole heart; suppose further that he has a commitment to this belief, that he has taken irrevocable actions because of it; finally, suppose that he is presented with evidence, unequivocal and undeniable evidence, that his belief is wrong; what will happen? The individual will frequently emerge, not only unshaken, but even more convinced of the truth of his beliefs than ever before. Indeed, he may even show a new fervour about convincing and converting other people to his view.

Denying reality in order to preserve a view of the world is not a practice confined to cults. Cognitive dissonance is the normal human condition. Messianic movements, whose followers live expecting the arrival of a saviour, embody this dissonance in a pure form. As Festinger writes, 'Ever since the crucifixion of Jesus, many Christians have hoped for the second coming of Christ, and movements predicting specific dates have not been rare . . . [Messianic believers] are convinced followers; they commit themselves by uprooting their lives . . . the Second Advent does not occur. And, we note, far from halting the movement, this disconfirmation gives it new life.' Apocalyptic movements need not be overtly religious. Citing Festinger's work, the literary critic Frank Kermode observed that, 'though for us the End has perhaps lost its naive imminence, its shadow still lies on the crises of our fictions.'

The shadow of apocalypse falls on many radical movements. Reproduced in secular form, apocalyptic myths possessed revolutionaries from the Jacobins to the Bolsheviks and beyond, inspiring movements as seemingly different as Trotskyism and late twentieth-century American neo-conservatism. Proletarian humanity in Soviet Russia, the *Übermensch* in Nazi Germany, the global producer-consumer awaited by congregations of the rich at meetings of the World Economic Forum in Davos – any one of these versions of humanity would have marked something new in history. Happily, the end-time failed to arrive and none of the phantoms materialized.

If there is anything unique about the human animal it is that it has the ability to grow knowledge at an accelerating rate while being chronically incapable of learning from experience. Science and technology are cumulative, whereas ethics and politics deal with recurring dilemmas. Whatever they are called, torture and slavery are universal evils; but these evils cannot be consigned to the past like redundant theories in science. They return under different names: torture as enhanced interrogation techniques, slavery as human trafficking. Any reduction in universal evils is an advance in civilization. But, unlike scientific knowledge, the restraints of civilized life cannot be stored on a computer disc. They are habits of behaviour, which once broken are hard to mend. Civilization is natural for humans, but so is barbarism.

The evidence of science and history is that humans are only ever partly and intermittently rational, but for modern humanists the solution is simple: human beings must in future be more reasonable. These enthusiasts for reason have not noticed that the idea that humans may one day be more rational requires a greater leap of faith than anything in religion. Since it requires a miraculous breach in the order of things, the idea that Jesus returned from the dead is not as contrary to reason as the notion that human beings will in future be different from how they have always been.

In the most general terms, humanism is the idea that the human animal is the site of some kind of unique value in the world. The philosophers of ancient Greece believed that humans were special in having a capacity for reason lacking in other animals, and some of these philosophers – notably Socrates, at least as he is described by Plato – believed that through the use of reason humans could access a spiritual realm. A related aspect of humanism is the idea that the human mind reflects the order of the cosmos. The spiritual realm in which Socrates may have believed was composed of timeless forms – in other words, metaphysical projections of human concepts. A third aspect of humanism is the idea that history is a story of human advance, with rationality increasing over time. This is a distinctively modern view, nowhere found among the wiser thinkers of the ancient world.

Not everyone who is described as a humanist has accepted these ideas. The sixteenth-century essayist Michel de Montaigne has been seen as a humanist because he turned to classical learning and a life of self-cultivation. But Montaigne mocked the belief that humans are superior to other animals, rejected the notion that the human mind mirrors the world and ridiculed the idea that it is reason that enables humans to live well. There is no trace in him of the belief in progress that would later shape modern humanism. As a good sceptic, Montaigne left open the window to faith. But there is nothing in his writings of the mystical ideas that underpin assertions of human uniqueness in Socrates and Plato.

Humanists today, who claim to take a wholly secular view of things, scoff at mysticism and religion. But the unique status of humans is hard to defend, and even to understand, when it is cut off from any idea of transcendence. In a strictly naturalistic view – one in which the world is taken on its own terms, without reference to a creator or any spiritual realm – there is no hierarchy of value with humans at the top. There are simply multifarious animals, each with their own needs. Human uniqueness is a myth inherited from religion, which humanists have recycled into science.

The hostility of humanists to myth is telling, since if anything is peculiarly human it is myth-making. Every human culture is animated by myth, in some degree, while no other animal displays anything similar. Humanists are also ruled by myths, though the ones by which they are possessed have none of the beauty or the wisdom of those that they scorn. The myth that human beings can use their minds to lift themselves out of the natural world, which in Socrates and Plato was part of a mystical philosophy, has been renewed in a garbled version of the language of evolution.

There is little in the current fad for evolutionary theories of society that cannot be found, sometimes more clearly expressed, in the writings of Herbert Spencer, the Victorian prophet of what would later be called Social Darwinism. Believing the human history was itself a kind of evolutionary process, Spencer asserted that the end-point of the process was laissez-faire capitalism. His disciples Sidney and Beatrice Webb, early members of the Fabian Society and admirers of the Soviet Union, believed it culminated in communism. Aiming to be more judicious, a later generation of theorists has nominated 'democratic capitalism' as the terminus. As might have been foreseen, none of these consummations has come to pass.

The most important feature of natural selection is that it is a process of drift. Evolution has no end-point or direction, so if the development of society is an evolutionary process it is one that is going nowhere. The destinations that successive generations of theorists have assigned to evolution have no basis in science. Invariably, they are the prevailing idea of progress recycled in Darwinian terms.

As refined by later scientists, Darwin's theory posits the natural selection of random genetic mutations. In contrast, no one has come up with a unit of selection or a mechanism through which evolution operates in society. On an evolutionary view the human mind has no built-in bias to truth or rationality and will continue to develop according to the imperative of survival. Theories of human rationality increasing through social evolution are as groundless today as they were when Spencer used them to promote laissez-faire capitalism and the Webbs communism. Reviving long-exploded errors, twenty-first-century believers in progress unwittingly demonstrate the unreality of progress in the history of ideas.

For humanists, denying that humanity can live without myths can only be a type of pessimism. They take for granted that if human beings came to be more like the rational figments they have in mind, the result would be an improvement. Leave aside the assumption – itself very questionable – that a rational life must be one without myths. Rational or not, life without myth is like life without art or sex – insipid and inhuman. The actuality, with all its horrors, is preferable. Luckily a choice need not be made, since the life of reason that humanists anticipate is only a fantasy.

If there is a choice it is between myths. In comparison with the Genesis myth, the modern myth in which humanity is marching to a better future is mere superstition. As the Genesis story teaches, knowledge cannot save us from ourselves. If we know more than before, it means only that we have greater scope to enact our fantasies. But – as the Genesis myth also teaches – there is no way we can rid ourselves of what we know. If we try to regain a state of innocence, the result can only be a worse madness. The message of Genesis is that in the most vital areas of human life there can be no progress, only an unending struggle with our own nature.

When contemporary humanists invoke the idea of progress they are mixing together two different myths: a Socratic myth of reason and a Christian myth of salvation. If the resulting body of ideas is incoherent, that is the source of its appeal. Humanists believe that humanity improves along with the growth of knowledge, but the belief that the increase of knowledge goes with advances in civilization is an act of faith. They see the realization of human potential as the goal of history, when rational inquiry shows history to have no goal. They exalt nature, while insisting that humankind – an accident of nature – can overcome the natural limits that shape the lives of other animals. Plainly absurd, this nonsense gives meaning to the lives of people who believe they have left all myths behind.

To expect humanists to give up their myths would be unreasonable. Like cheap music, the myth of progress lifts the spirits as it numbs the brain. The fact that rational humanity shows no sign of ever arriving only makes humanists cling more fervently to the conviction that humankind will someday be redeemed from unreason. Like believers in flying saucers, they interpret the non-event as confirming their faith.

Science and the idea of progress may seem joined together, but the end-result of progress in science is to show the impossibility of progress in civilization. Science is a solvent of illusion, and among the illusions it dissolves are those of humanism. Human knowledge increases, while human irrationality stays the same. Scientific inquiry may be an embodiment of reason, but what such inquiry demonstrates is that humans are not rational animals. The fact that humanists refuse to accept the demonstration only confirms its truth.

Atheism and humanism may also seem to be conjoined when in fact they are at odds. Among contemporary atheists, disbelief in progress is a type of blasphemy. Pointing to the flaws of the human animal has become an act of sacrilege. The decline of religion has only stiffened the hold of faith on the mind. Unbelief today should begin by questioning not religion but secular faith. A type of atheism that refused to revere humanity would be a genuine advance. Freud's thought exemplifies atheism of this kind; but Freud has been rejected precisely because he refused to flatter the human animal. It is not surprising that atheism remains a humanist cult. To suppose that the myth of progress could be shaken off would be to ascribe to modern humanity a capacity for improvement even greater than that which it ascribes to itself.

Modern myths are myths of salvation stated in secular terms. What both kinds of myths have in common is that they answer to a need for meaning that cannot be denied. In order to survive, humans have invented science. Pursued consistently, scientific inquiry acts to undermine myth. But life without myth is impossible, so science has become a channel for myths – chief among them, a myth of salvation through science. When truth is at odds with meaning, it is meaning that wins. Why this should be so is a delicate question. Why is meaning so important? Why do humans need a reason to live? Is it because they could not endure life if they did not believe it contained hidden significance? Or does the demand for meaning come from attaching too much sense to language – from thinking that our lives are books we have not yet learnt to read?

2 Beyond the Last Thought

The chief defect of humanism is that it concerns
human beings. Between humanism and something else, it might be possible to create an accept-
able fiction.

Wallace Stevens

FREUD'S CIGARS AND THE
LONG WAY ROUND TO NIRVANA

When Freud invented psychoanalysis he believed he
was founding a new science, a branch of neurology.
In fact he was renewing an immemorial inquiry into
how human beings should live. Freud – paradoxi-
cally, a thoroughly modern thinker – planted a
question mark over modern ideals. Without surren-
dering his resolute atheism, he reformulated one of
the central insights of religion: humans are cracked

vessels. The obstacles to human fulfilment are not only in the world around us. Humans harbour impulses that sabotage fulfilment in themselves. *Eros* – love, or creativity – is an integral part of being human; but so, Freud thought, is *thanatos*, the death instinct that finds expression in hate and destruction. The aim of therapy was not to bring peace to these warring impulses, or to secure the victory of one over the other, but to effect a change in the mind through which both could be accepted.

In believing that humans are in need of an inner change, Freud was continuing a tradition that has existed, in one form or another, for as long as humans have existed. Through all of history and pre-history it has been accepted that there is something wrong with the human animal. Health may be the natural condition of other species, but in humans it is sickness that is normal. To be chronically unwell is part of what it means to be human. It is no accident that every culture has its own versions of therapy. Tribal shamans and modern psychotherapists answer the same needs and practise the same trade.

Freud is sometimes accused of creating a culture in which every human difficulty is approached as a problem in psychological adjustment. The accusation is revealing, since it shows how the central thrust of Freud's work continues to be resisted. What marks off Freud's from earlier therapies and from those that came after him is that he does not offer to heal the soul. Over the past century, partly as a side-effect of Freud's work, the normal conflicts of the mind have come to be seen as ailments that can be remedied. For Freud, on the other hand, it is the hope of a life without conflict that ails us. Along with every serious philosophy and religion, Freud accepted that humans are sickly animals. Where he was original was in also accepting that the human sickness has no cure.

It would not be wrong to see Freud as fashioning a new type of Stoic ethics. A mark of his iconoclasm is that he viewed resignation as a virtue. Aiming to arm the individual against the world, he knew that the world would in the end win. With the Stoics, he accepted that humans cannot be masters of their destiny. Not choice but fate decides when and where we will be born, who are our parents, what circumstances shape our lives and how much we suffer. Yet there is still the possibility of a certain freedom. The Roman Stoic Seneca defined this freedom in a letter: 'I have set freedom before my eyes; and I am striving for that reward. And what is freedom, you ask? It means not being a slave to any circumstance, to any constraint, to any chance; it means compelling Fortune to enter the lists on equal terms.'

Modern thinkers tend to believe that human beings can decide their fates, which is much the same as believing that there is no such thing as fate. Freud joins the ancients in accepting that our lives are shaped by fate, while also affirming that we can shape the stance we adopt towards our fate. Yet it is too simple to think of Freud as a Stoic out of season.

Finding his duties a burden, the Stoic emperor Marcus Aurelius (AD 121–80) consoled himself with the thought that each person had a place in the scheme of things. Like the Christians who believed the universe was shaped by a divine *Logos*, Marcus found peace in submitting to the cosmos. Freud had no interest in submitting to an extra-human order, natural or divine. He refused the consolations of the Stoics, along with those offered by the Christians and their disciples, the humanist believers in progress. He accepted chaos as final, and in this he was modern. At the same time his distance from modern ideals is clear. Psychoanalysis has been seen as promoting personal autonomy, when the opposite is more nearly true. Echoing the Christian faith in free will, humanists hold that human beings are – or may someday become – free to choose their lives. They forget that the self that does the choosing has not itself been chosen.

Freud's teaching has as much to do with the helplessness all human beings experience as infants as it has with repressed sexuality. He is telling us that our early experiences leave indelible marks. Through the practice of psychotherapy these marks may be seen more clearly, but they cannot be effaced. The end of psychoanalysis – an interminable process, Freud warned – is the acceptance of a personal fate.

This sounds like a Stoic philosophy. But if Freud rejected the Stoic view of the universe, he also rejected a Stoic view of ethics. For Stoics such as Marcus Aurelius, the good life was a life of virtue. To transgress morality in order to live a better life was unthinkable, since the commands and prohibitions of morality were the laws of the universe turned into principles of conduct. Not believing in a law-governed cosmos, Freud took a different view. Morality was a set of human conventions, which could be disregarded or altered when it stood in the way of a more satisfying life. It was not just the unconscious that had to be mastered. So did the super-ego, the part of the human mind called the conscience, which would like to be entirely 'good'. The super-ego – in German, *das Über-Ich*, or 'Over-I' – internalizes the constraints of civilization. But in Freud's view it is only when they have achieved a certain detachment from 'morality' that anyone can claim to be an individual.

Like Nietzsche but more soberly, Freud envisioned a form of life that was 'beyond good and evil'. Describing the qualities of a good psychoanalyst in a letter to a colleague, he wrote that a good psychoanalyst should not be too moral: 'Your analysis suffers from the hereditary weakness of virtue. It is the work of an over-decent man . . . One has to be a bad fellow, transcend the rules, sacrifice oneself, betray, and behave like the artist who buys paints with his wife's household money, or burns the furniture to warm the room for his model. Without such criminality there is no real achievement.'

One of the goals of psychoanalysis was the taming of morality. Not only anarchic impulse but also the moral sense had to submit to reason. But the dictatorship of reason could never be complete. If our impulses are at war with each other they are also at war with the demands of conscience, themselves often conflicting. The strength of the ego is shown not in trying to harmonize these conflicts but in learning to live with them. That is part of what it means to accept a personal fate. But, for Freud, fatalism had nothing to do with passivity.

In some ways Freud's view of human life resembles that of Arthur Schopenhauer, the nineteenth-century German philosopher of pessimism. Freud claimed not to have read Schopenhauer until late in life. But he also acknowledged that Schopenhauer had anticipated the fundamental insight of psychoanalysis, writing: 'Probably very few people can have realized the momentous significance for life and science of the recognition of unconscious mental processes. It was not psychoanalysis, however, let us hasten to add, which took the first step. There are famous philoso-phers who may be cited as forerunners – above all the great thinker Schopenhauer, whose unconscious "Will" is equivalent to the mental instincts of psycho-analysis.' Schopenhauer also recognized sexuality as the prime moving force in human life. 'Sexual desire is the ultimate goal of almost all human effort,' Scho-penhauer wrote. 'It knows how to slip its love-notes and ringlets even into ministerial portfolios and philo-sophical manuscripts.' These observations could well have come from Freud.

Both thinkers parted company with the dominant western tradition in accepting that it is not the con-scious mind that shapes human life. Beneath what we imagine are our choices, it is unconscious will that rules us. At bottom the world itself is will, a field of energy that finds expression as bodily desire. Borrow-ing the term from a former colleague, the 'wild psychoanalyst' George Groddeck, Freud called this inner flow of energy the id (in German, 'it'). Groddeck had taken the term from Nietzsche, but Nietzsche took the idea from Schopenhauer. Freud's id is Schopenhauer's will, a metaphysical category turned into a psychological theory.

For Schopenhauer as for Freud the world is an arena of unending struggle. But Schopenhauer offers a possibility of redemption, and it is here that Freud parts company with him. While believing that human autonomy was an illusion, Schopenhauer at the same time held out the prospect of liberation from illusion. Salvation lies in shaking off the ego, making possible a way of life based on an 'oceanic feeling of oneness'.

Freud did not share this dream of salvation. The possibility of escape from illusion that Schopenhauer held out was itself an illusion. The oceanic feeling was real enough, but it could not be the basis for a way of living. Whatever moments of release they might experience, humans were fated to a life of struggle. 'Where id was,' Freud wrote, 'there shall ego be.' The sense of oneness had no magic for him. Human life may be a meandering road to death. But, until we reach our destination, we are at war.

A type of resignation was the core of Freud's ethic. But the resignation he advised was the opposite of submission to the world. He never envisioned merging the self with any cosmic order. Resignation meant accepting the fact of ultimate chaos. Like the Stoics Freud knew that much had to be renounced if the mind was not to be always wavering. Yet his goal was not the tranquillity pursued – and never found, one suspects – by Marcus Aurelius. Instead Freud suggested a way of life based on accepting perpetual unrest. Resignation did not mean shrinking the self to the point where it could live without being thwarted by fate. It meant fortifying the self so that human beings could assert themselves against fate.

Freud practised this active fatalism in his own life. When, after staying in Nazi-occupied Austria until it was almost too late, he finally left his homeland, he was required by the Gestapo to sign a document testifying that he had had every opportunity 'to live and work in full freedom' and had 'not the slightest reason for any complaint'. He signed the document, adding an ironic codicil of his own: 'I can most highly recommend the Gestapo to anyone.' Relying on the Gestapo's inability to perceive that they were being mocked, it was a gesture of reckless defiance.

So, in another way, was Freud's refusal to give up cigars. Throughout his last years in Vienna, then in London, he continued smoking – 'a protection and a weapon in the combat of life' – despite having as part of treatment for cancer a painful prosthesis inserted in his jaw, which he had to lever open to insert his cigars. Near the end of his illness, when he could no longer smoke, he described his life as 'a small island of pain floating in an ocean of indifference'. When Freud's faithful disciple Ernest Jones came to say goodbye to the dying man, Freud 'opened his eyes, recognized me and waved his hand, then dropped it with a highly expressive gesture'. The gesture, Jones wrote, conveyed 'a wealth of meaning:

greetings, farewell, resignation. It said as plainly as possible, "The rest is silence."' Some days later Freud's doctor, honouring a promise he had made, administered the doses of morphine that ended Freud's suffering.

Freud did not shun pleasure in order to avoid pain. Better enjoy one's pleasures to the end, he seems to have thought, than suffer a life of painless ease. When his cancer became unbearable he opted for assisted suicide. His life was an example of human will being asserted against fate. But he never imagined that fate could be overcome, which is why this most wilful individual counselled resignation.

The founder of psychoanalysis has been seen as providing a therapy for modern ills, when what he actually did is subvert modern myths of health. But Freud was not suggesting that the mind could be emptied of myth. Psychoanalysis was itself a kind of mythology – 'our mythological theory of instincts', as Freud put it in an exchange on the causes of war he had with Einstein. Freud writes that the death instinct – an instinct that is 'at work in every living creature and is striving to bring it to ruin and to reduce life to its original condition of inanimate matter' – may be a myth. 'It may perhaps seem to you as though our theories are a kind of mythology,' he writes to Einstein, 'and, in the present case, not even an agreeable one.' Then he goes on to ask Einstein: 'But does not every science come in the end to a mythology like this? Cannot the same be said today of your own Physics?'

Freud's admission that psychoanalysis was a kind of myth was echoed by the Spanish-American philosopher George Santayana. In an essay he entitled 'A Long Way Round to Nirvana' (1933), Santayana discussed Freud's idea that human life is ruled by the rival instincts of *eros* and *thanatos*:

These new myths of Freud's about life, like his old ones about dreams, are calculated to enlighten and to chasten us enormously about ourselves. The human spirit, when it awakes, finds itself in trouble; it is burdened, for no reason it can assign, with all sorts of anxieties about food, pressures, noises and pains. It is born, as another myth has it, in original sin . . . The same insight is contained in another wise myth which has inspired morality and religion in India from time immemorial: I mean the doctrine of Karma. We are born, it says, with a heritage, a character imposed, and a long task assigned, all due to the ignorance which in our past lives has led us into all sorts of commitments . . . Some philosophers without self-knowledge think that the variations and entanglements that the future may bring are manifestations of spirit; but they are, as Freud has indicated, imposed on living beings by external pressure, and take shape in the realm of matter . . . Deep and dark as the soul may be when you look at it from outside, it is something perfectly natural; and the same understanding that can unearth our suppressed young passions, and dispel our stubborn bad habits, can show us where our true good lies. Nature has marked out the path for us beforehand; there are snares in it, but also primroses, and it leads to peace.

Santayana goes on to quote Freud in *Beyond the Pleasure Principle* (1920), where Freud interprets the death instinct as a tendency of all living matter: 'An instinct would be a tendency in living organic matter impelling it towards reinstatement of an earlier condition . . . It would be counter to the conservative nature of instinct if the goal of life were a state never hitherto reached. It must rather be an ancient starting point, which the living being left long ago, and to which it harks back again by all the circuitous paths of development . . . The goal of all life is death . . .'

Citing this passage, Santayana recognized that Freud was giving voice to a new myth. The idea that organisms live in order to die is not a claim that science can prove or disprove. The method of modern science is to understand the natural world without ever invoking goals or purposes. And yet, Santayana goes on,

> the suggestion conveyed by Freud's speculations is true. In what sense can myths be true or false? In the sense that, in terms drawn from moral predicaments or from literary psychology, they may report the general movement and the pertinent issue of material facts, and may inspire us with a wise sentiment in their presence. In this sense I should say that Greek mythology was true and Calvinist theology was false. The chief terms employed in psychoanalysis have always been metaphorical: 'unconscious wishes', 'the pleasure-principle', 'the Oedipus complex', 'Narcissism', 'the censor'; nevertheless, interesting and profound vistas may be opened up, and a fresh start may be made with fewer encumbrances and less morbid inhibitions.

Using Santayana's distinctions, Freud's mythology of the death instinct is true in the way that Greek myth is true, while the modern myth of progress is false in the way that Calvinist theology is false. Sounding as archaic as Greek myth – no one in polite society dares speak of instincts today – Freud's mythology captures features of human experience that are enduring and universal. Of course Freud's ideas are a system of metaphors. So is all human discourse, even if metaphors are not all of one kind. Science is not distinguished from myth by science being literally true and myth only a type of poetic analogy. While their aims are different, both are composed of symbols we use to deal with a slippery world.

When Freud founded psychoanalysis he thought that human behaviour could be studied like any natural phenomenon. Yet the upshot of his work is that we are obliged to admit that our knowledge of ourselves cannot be other than highly limited. Shaped by an animal struggle for life, the human view of the world is haphazard and slanting. For all we know, science could be a succession of lucky errors. Self-knowledge is even more problematic. If we learn something new about a star, the star does not change; but when we discover something new about ourselves, we alter the person we have come to be.

This need not be discouraging, Freud suggests. If we can retrieve some of what has been lost we will see ourselves in a different way. From the fragments that emerge from a past that has been repressed, it is possible to envision other lives you could have lived. Among these there may be one that for a time you adopt as your own. Learning how you came to be what you have been, you can shift your shape as you go along.

FROM ILLUSIONS TO FICTIONS

Freud's acknowledgement that psychoanalysis was – in part at least – an exercise in myth-making shows his distance from the main current of western philosophy, including Schopenhauer. While he denied that reason could ever direct human life, Schopenhauer was still a metaphysician in the classical tradition. Even though what could be said was nearly all negative, he wanted to say something about the world as it is in itself. In contrast Freud, whose thinking was shaped by post-metaphysical Viennese philosophy of the kind promoted by the physicist Ernst Mach (1838–1916), tried to avoid making claims about things-in-themselves.

Mach inspired the philosophy later known as Logical Positivism, which held that science is the model for every kind of human knowledge. According to Mach the only thing humans can know is their own sensations, and it is from these that the edifice of science is built. Freud shared Mach's view and wanted to be a scientist himself. But there is a tension at the centre of this philosophy, which Freud inherited and never fully resolved. In Mach's view science was a device for ordering human sensations. But in serving this function science is not radically different from other modes of thought. In that case science and myth, though in some ways different, cannot be fundamentally at odds.

When Freud opposed science against myth he over-looked the fact that he later invoked in his conversation with Einstein: science and myth are both ways of dealing with the chaos of sensation. He continued to believe that only science produced anything that could be called knowledge. Everything else was just illusion. At the same time he came to think that illusions were not just errors. Serving the human need for meaning, illusion had a place in life, and so did myth. Science itself had some of the attributes of mythology. But if this is so then purging the mind of myth, which at times Freud saw as the aim of psychoanalysis, is impossible. A life without myths is itself the stuff of myth.

For most of his life Freud aimed to extend the reach of conscious awareness. For this Freud, reli-gion was the primary example of the human need for illusion. But as a later Freud came to realize, the illu-sions of religion contain truths that cannot be conveyed in other ways.

In *The Future of an Illusion* (1927) Freud wrote:

An illusion is not the same as an error, nor is it nec-essarily an error . . . In other words, we refer to a belief as an illusion when wish-fulfilment plays a prominent role in its motivation, and in the process we disregard its relationship to reality, just as the illusion itself dispenses with such accreditations . . .

If, armed with this information, we return to the teachings of religion, we may say again: they are all illusions, unverifiable . . . Some of them are so improbable, so contrary to everything we have learnt so laboriously about the world, that (making due allowance for psychological differences) they can be likened to delusions. The reality value of most of them cannot be assessed. Just as they are unverifiable, they are also irrefutable. Too little is known as yet to bring them into critical focus. The world's riddles unveil themselves only slowly to our researches; there are many questions science cannot yet answer. However, as we see it, scientific work is the sole avenue that can lead to knowledge of the reality outside ourselves.

At this point in Freud's thinking science and religion could only be rivals. If science serves the demand for knowledge, religion serves the need for meaning. Illusions may be useful, even humanly indispensable. But that does not make them true, Freud insisted. He spurned the 'as-if' philosophy that his contemporary Hans Vaihinger presented in his book *Philosophie des Als Ob* (*The Philosophy of 'As If'*) in which all of human thought consists of fictions:

there are plenty of assumptions in our intellectual activity that we quite agree are unfounded, even absurd. They are called fictions, but for a variety of reasons we allegedly have to act 'as if' we believed those fictions. This (we are told) applies with regard to the teachings of religion because of their incomparable importance in sustaining human society. This line of argument is not far removed from the *credo quia absurdum*. However, in my opinion the 'as-if' demand is one that only a philosopher can make. Anyone whose thinking is not influenced by the arts of philosophy will never be able to accept it; so far as he is concerned the admission of absurdity, of being contrary to reason, is the end of the matter.

To propose that we believe something because it is absurd – as the third-century Christian theologian Tertullian did when he invented the slogan *Credo quia absurdum* (I believe because it is absurd), which Freud cites – is itself absurd, an exercise in conscious self-deception that is bound to fail. How can we live on the basis of fictions? In Freud's view, it is humanly impossible: 'No, our science is not an illusion. What would be an illusion would be to think we might obtain elsewhere that which science cannot give us.' In the Positivist philosophy that Freud follows here, myths are primitive theories that have been falsified by science. But the difference between myths, illusions and fictions on the one hand and science on the other is less clear, even in Freud's own thinking, than he recognized.

Freud is adamant that science is not fiction, and it is true that the methods of science include falsification – the systematic attempt to demonstrate that a theory is in error – whereas myths and fictions cannot be true or false. But if we know anything from the history of science, it is that the most severely tested theories still contain errors. No doubt the theories we use are the ones we think closest to the truth; but we do not know which parts of them are true and which are not. Still we go on using them. It has been said that myths are fictions whose human authorship is not acknowledged. But scientific theories can also become myths when their fictive qualities are forgotten.

Vaihinger, who first advanced the idea that all human thought is composed of fictions, distinguished clearly between the fictions of science and those of poetry and religion:

We must indicate the boundaries which separate scientific fiction from what is also designated by the same term.

Fictio means, in the first place, an activity of *fingere*, that is to say, of constructing, forming, giving shape, elaborating, presenting, artistically fashioning; conceiving, thinking, imagining, assuming, planning, devising, inventing. Secondly, it refers to the product of these activities, the fictional assumption, fabrication, created, the imagined case. Its most conspicuous character is that of unhampered and free expression.

Mythology, insofar as it may be regarded as the common mother of religion, poetry, art and science, shows us the first expression in free constructive activity of the inventive faculty, of imagination and of fantasy. It is here that we first find products of fantasy which do not correspond with reality.

If we accept Vaihinger's account, science and myth are not one and the same: their methods are different, and so are the needs they serve. But science and myth are alike in being makeshifts that humans erect as shelters from a world they cannot know. The hard and fast distinction between science and other modes of thought that Freud wanted to maintain turns out to be blurred and shifting.

The changing distinctions Freud made between science and religion show how unstable the boundaries between them became. He was never tempted by any religion. His atheism, along with his suspicion of modern ideals, was firmly entrenched. Yet he came to think that religion had an irreplaceable role in human development – not least in making psychoanalysis possible. In *Moses and Monotheism* (1939), his last book, he argued that it is to monotheism that we may owe our knowledge of the unconscious mind. If psychoanalysis is a science, it is one that owes its existence to the greatest illusion of all.

Freud's account of the history of religion is refreshingly unorthodox. He suggests that Christianity, which is usually seen as a major advance in human thought, was a step backwards. With its ban on images of the deity, Judaism gave birth to the idea of an invisible reality. At this point a type of introspection became possible that had not existed before. If God is invisible the inner world might be unknown to us just like that unseen God. It was Christianity that introduced the notion that God resembles humans – even, in the myth of incarnation, becoming one of them. God was then no longer an invisible presence but a divine personage, which could be known with as much certainty as we know ourselves. The possibility that much of our inner world might be hidden from us was lost.

Another obstacle was the Socratic tradition. The type of self-examination promoted by Socrates is quite different from that practised in psychoanalysis. As portrayed by Plato, Socrates believed that the human mind was like the cosmos in obeying laws of logic and ethics: if you understand yourself, you are bound to be good. Freud makes no such assumption. The secret workings of the mind are ignorant of logic

– the id, Freud says, knows nothing of the law that forbids self-contradiction – and are indifferent to right and wrong. Claiming to be the pursuit of truth, Socratic self-examination was the working out of a myth.

Freud's assault on illusion was directed against religion, but his implicit attack on secular mythology was more deadly. The myth of progress is the chief consolation of modern humankind. But Freud did not aim to provide another version of consolation. If he had an aim, it may have been to explore what it would mean to live without consolations. Freud is the thinker who poses the question: how can modern humans beings live without modern myths?

THE SUPREME FICTION

The end of thought seems to be unending doubt. Facing this situation, the poet Wallace Stevens suggested that we put our trust in fictions: 'The final belief is to believe in a fiction, which you know to be a fiction, there being nothing else. The exquisite truth is to know that it is a fiction and to believe in it willingly.'

Stevens devoted one of his greatest poems to exploring what this might mean. 'Notes toward a

Supreme Fiction' is not a chain of argumentation.
The poet has no interest in persuasion. In the poem
Stevens poses what he regarded as the final issue of
thought:

> It must
> Be possible . . .
> To find the real,
> To be stripped of every fiction except one,
> The fiction of an absolute . . .

To be stripped of every fiction except the fiction of
an absolute is to find your mind at 'a point / Beyond
which thought could not progress as thought'. At
that point, Stevens seems to suggest, one must simply
choose. But how can anyone choose among fictions?
How can anyone believe in something they know is
not true? As Freud noted, the conscious choice of a
fiction is like Tertullian's *Credo quia absurdum* – I
believe because it is absurd. Freud thought such a
choice impossible. Yet a life based on fictions cannot
be impossible, since we live such a life every day. We
may not choose the fictions by which we live, or not
consciously. Our lives turn on fictions all the same.

The confusion is in the idea of belief. We are
accustomed to think our lives stand on beliefs about
ourselves and the world: science is a search for true
beliefs and religion the sum of our beliefs about

ultimate things. In this way of thinking, a relic of western philosophy, belief is all important. Stevens falls into this ancient confusion when he writes of believing in a fiction willingly. He wanted 'to stick to the nicer knowledge of belief, that what it believes in is not true'. But fictions are not conscious falsehoods. Creations of the imagination, they are neither true nor false. We cannot do without an idea of truth. Things go their own way however we think of them. But we can live without believing our fictions to be facts. We need not always be patching our view of things to shut out a dissonant world.

An anxious attachment to belief is the chief weakness of the western mind. It is a fixation with a long lineage, going all the way back to Socrates, the founder of philosophy – at least as we understand it (and him) today. But outside of some currents in western religion and the humanist successors of monotheism, belief is not the foundation of practice. Religions have produced highly refined systems of ideas, such as Vedanta, Buddhist dialectics and the Kabbalah, but these are not apologies for belief. If they have a practical task, it is to point to realities that cannot be captured in beliefs. In this they resemble Stevens's fictions.

A supreme fiction, Stevens tells us, must have a number of attributes: it must be abstract; it must change; and it must give pleasure. These are interesting requirements. Though they develop over time, myths are thought to be timeless. Why not admit the obvious, Stevens seems to be asking, and accept that the fictions that shape our lives are as changeable as our lives are themselves? It may seem odd to ask of a fiction that it give pleasure. But why else should anyone make it a part of their life? A fiction is not something you need to justify. When it comes to you, you accept it freely. As for other people, they can do as they please.

The supreme fiction is not any final belief but the activity of making fictions, which Stevens calls poetry. Fictions cannot be created at will. If they could be called into being as we wish, they could also be dismissed whenever we like. That is the project of humanism. But while the fictions by which we live are human creations, they are beyond human control. Like the golden bird singing in the palm in Stevens's poem 'Of Mere Being', they come:

> at the end of the mind,
> Beyond the last thought . . .
> The bird sings. Its feathers shine.

The mere being of which Stevens speaks is the pure emptiness to which our fictions may sometimes point. Emerging in ways beyond understanding, our most important fictions are a kind of fate; but not a fate that is the same for everybody. No fiction could be supreme for everyone, or even for a single person, for ever. The supreme fiction is not the one idea worth having, for there can be no such idea.

Admitting that our lives are shaped by fictions may give a kind of freedom – possibly the only kind that human beings can attain. Accepting that the world is without meaning, we are liberated from confinement in the meaning we have made. Knowing there is nothing of substance in our world may seem to rob that world of value. But this nothingness may be our most precious possession, since it opens to us the world that exists beyond ourselves.

HAPPINESS, A FICTION YOU CAN DO WITHOUT

Freud wrote to one of his patients: 'I do not doubt that it would be easier for fate to take away your suffering than it would be for me. But you will see for yourself how much has been gained if we succeed in turning your hysterical misery into common unhappiness. Having restored your inner life, you will be better able to arm yourself against that unhappiness.' For Freud the pursuit of happiness is a distraction from living. It would be better to aim for something different – a type of life in which you do not need a fantasy of satisfaction in order to find being human an interesting and worthwhile experience.

The contemporary creed is that fulfilment can be found by being the person you truly want to be. Within each of us there are unique possibilities, waiting to be developed. Our misfortune is that these possibilities are mostly thwarted. Hence, we like to think, the sadly stifled lives many people lead; they have missed the chance to be themselves. But do they know who it is that they want to be? If they became that person, would they then be 'happy'? Only someone who was chronically miserable would base their lives on such a far-fetched speculation. As it is, most spend their lives in a state of hopeful turmoil. They find meaning in the suffering that the struggle for happiness brings. In its flight from emptiness, modern humanity is attached to nothing so much as this state of happy misery.

The ideal of self-realization owes much to the Romantic movement. For the Romantics the supreme achievement was originality. In creating new forms the artist was godlike. The poems and paintings of Romantic artists were not variations on traditional themes. They were meant to be something new in the world, and soon it came to be believed that every human life could be original in this way. Only by finding and becoming their true self could anyone be happy.

For Freud there was no true self to be found. The

mind was a chaos, and imposing order on it was the task of reason. Writing in 1932 to Einstein, who had asked him whether war could ever be abolished, Freud wrote: 'The ideal condition of course would be a community of men who had subordinated their instinctual life to the dictatorship of reason. Nothing else could unite men so completely and tenaciously, even if there were no emotional ties between them. But in all probability that is a Utopian expectation.'

For Freud human life was a process of ego-building, not the quest for a fictitious inner self. Looking for your true self invites unending disappointment. If you have no special potential, the cost of trying to bring your inner nature to fruition will be a painfully mis-spent existence. Even if you have unusual talent, it will only bring fulfilment if others also value it. Few human beings are as unhappy as those who have a gift that no one wants. Anyway, who wants to spend their life hanging around waiting to be recognized? As John Ashbery wrote:

> A talent for self-realisation
> Will get you only so far as the vacant lot
> Next to the lumber yard, where they have
>   rollcall.

The Romantic ideal tells people to seek their true self. There is no such self, but that does not mean we can be anything we want to be. Talent is a gift of fortune, not something that can be chosen. Imagining that you have talent that you lack turns you into a version of the composer Salieri, whose life was poisoned by the appearance of Mozart. Salieri was not without ability. For much of his life he enjoyed a successful career. But if we accept how he has been portrayed by Pushkin and others, Salieri was consumed by the suspicion that he was himself a fake. A society of people who have been taught to be themselves cannot be other than full of fakes.

The idea of self-realization is one of the most destructive of modern fictions. It suggests you can flourish in only one sort of life, or a small number of similar lives, when in fact everybody can thrive in a large variety of ways. We think of a happy life as one that culminates in eventual fulfilment. Ever since Aristotle philosophers have encouraged us to think in this backward-looking way. But it means thinking of your life as if it had already ended, and none of us knows how we will end. Spending your days writing an obituary of a person you might have been seems an odd way to live.

Human beings are more likely to find ways of living well if they do not spend their lives aiming to be happy. This is not to say we should pursue happiness indirectly – an idea also inherited from Aristotle. Rather, we are best off not looking for happiness at all. Looking for happiness is like having lived your life before it is over. You know everything important in advance: what you want, who you are. Why saddle yourself with the burden of being a character in such a dull tale? Better make up your life as you go along, and not be too attached to the stories you tell yourself on the way.

Learning to know yourself means telling the story of your life in a way that is more imaginative than before. As you come to see your life in the light of this new story, you will yourself change. Your life will then be shaped, you could say, by a new fiction. Framing these fictions was what Freud meant by the work of ego-building. The ego is itself a fiction, one that is never fixed or finished. 'In the realm of fiction,' Freud wrote, 'we find the plurality of lives which we need.'

JUNG'S ARYAN UNCONSCIOUS, OR WHAT MYTHS ARE NOT

Freud held back from considering ways in which myth might be renewed. His errant colleague Carl Jung had shown where that led. Jung's thought is interesting not because it has any value in itself, but for showing how psychology can become the vehicle for a new religion – a development that Freud always resisted. With Jung the therapist became a modern conductor of souls into the underworld. But the underworld into which Jung wanted to take humanity was his own invention, which he devised partly in order to obscure his behaviour in the years when Nazism seemed about to conquer Europe.

Jung's ideas about myth did not originate with him or with Freud. Preceding Jung's encounter with psychoanalysis, they were part of the intellectual ferment of late nineteenth-century and early twentieth-century Germany. At that time, occultist and theosophical sects and movements trying to develop a science-based evolutionary religion were powerful forces. The leading figure in this project was Ernst Haeckel (1834–1919), a professor of zoology at the University of Jena who commanded an enormous following in the German-speaking world. Haeckel's project was the creation of a new religion grounded in scientific materialism and evolutionary theory, which he called Monism. More responsible than any other thinker for the spread of Darwinism in Europe and the inventor of the science of ecology, Haeckel also promoted the idea that the human species was made up of a hierarchy of racial groups, while applied eugenics could enhance the quality of the population. These ideas would be the unifying creed of a pantheist church, which would supplant Christianity.

By the turn of the century there were Monist groups all over central Europe. Joined together in

1906 in a Monist League led by Haeckel, they included the founder of Positivism Ernst Mach, numerous Darwinian scientists, one of the founders of modern sociology Ferdinand Tönnies and the influential occultist Rudolf Steiner. A number of figures who later became prominent figures in the German communist party were members, as were some who became Nazis. Haeckel was a member of the Thule Society, a secret organization of radical nationalists to which Rudolf Hess, later Hitler's deputy, also belonged. After the Second World War, Haeckel would be celebrated as an intellectual hero in the communist German Democratic Republic.

For these figures an evolutionary religion was extremely attractive. Having in common a virulent hostility to Christian and Jewish traditions (many, including Haeckel himself, were explicitly anti-Semitic), they wanted a new religion in which modern science would be combined with ancient modes of thinking. Haeckel believed that conscious thought was grounded in archaic mental processes. Other thinkers connected with *völkisch* movements, who longed for a return of the 'organic' cultures they believed had existed in the past, promoted the idea that whole peoples have souls. *Volk* – etymologically linked with the English word 'folk' – meant a community or way of life that had not been disturbed by critical thought. Reviving this imaginary

folk-world meant expelling or otherwise neutraliz-
ing minorities that might disturb the communal
peace. Like all utopias, the *völkisch* dream required
the repression of disruptive elements.

It was from this milieu that Jung first picked up the
idea of the collective unconscious, a repository of
archetypal images that appeared in the mind as dreams
or visions. Retrieving these images and the myths they
embody from the unconscious became one of the goals
of the type of psychotherapy that Jung promoted after
his break with Freud. Rather than being a practice in
which individuals could frame their own myths, the
psychotherapist would connect the patient with myths
that were archetypal. Appearing in Gnostic texts and
in the arcane symbolism of alchemy, these eternal realities could be reintegrated into the modern psyche. The
result would be a state of mental unity in which conflicting forces were absorbed into a harmonious whole.

The exact nature of Jung's collective unconscious
remains a matter of dispute. In later writings Jung
maintained that it was universally human, but in
some of his earlier work he suggested that different
human groups had different kinds of unconscious
mind. 'The Aryan unconscious', he declared in a lecture to the Berlin Psychoanalytical Institute after it
had been taken over by Mathius Göring, Hermann
Göring's cousin, following the Nazi seizure of power,
'has a higher potential than the Jewish.'

In 1936 Jung published an article entitled 'Wotan', where he interpreted the rise of Nazism as an eruption of the ancient god of storm and frenzy. In the article he held back from endorsing the upheaval that was under way in Germany, hinting that it could be highly destructive. By 1943 his stance had tilted towards the Allies. Through the mediation of an American patient, Mary Bancroft, a former debutante, socialite and lover of Allen Dulles, who represented the OSS (Office of Strategic Services) in Switzerland and was later director of the CIA, Jung had become a source for American intelligence. In this capacity he worked as a profiler of the Nazi leaders while acting, according to some accounts, as a channel through which contact could be maintained with some of the moving forces in plots against Hitler. Most likely the full truth cannot be known, but the suspicion must be that throughout much of the Nazi period Jung was hedging his bets.

Jung's attitude to Nazism was shaped in part by the conviction that a new religion was needed to heal the modern soul. Here Jung's difference with Freud is stark and irreconcilable. In an exchange of letters with Jung in 1910 in which Jung suggested that psychoanalysis must 'transform Christ back into the soothsaying god of the vine', Freud wrote: 'But you mustn't regard me as the founder of a religion. My intentions are not so far-reaching . . . I am not thinking of a substitute for a religion: this need must be sublimated.'

Unlike Jung, Freud never claimed to heal the soul. Inner division was the price of being human. The split within the soul came, in large part, from the repression of desire; but Freud never imagined that repression could be avoided. A loss of instinctual satisfaction came with any kind of civilized life. But, for Freud, barbarism was not an attractive alternative.

Like Jung, Freud viewed interwar Europe as having descended into mass psychosis. Unlike Jung, he never welcomed this development. The forces that were released during this period were not numinous powers emerging from an unconscious repository of mythic wisdom. They were repressed impulses liberated from inner restraint. Without the ruin of bourgeois life by economic collapse, Nazism might never have developed into the hideously destructive force that it became. For many in interwar Europe, however, Nazism had a positive appeal on account of the promise of barbarism that it held out. Freud understood this appeal, but that did not mean he shared it. Modern civilization might be sickly, but so was the human animal. Embracing madness would not make the soul whole.

The difference between Jung and Freud is not that Jung celebrated myth while Freud wanted to rid the mind of it, though at times Freud did. It is that they had different understandings of myth. The myth-making impulse, which for Jung connected humans to a spiritual realm, was for Freud a natural capacity. If human life requires repression, it also needs myth. Repression means more than inhibiting the expression of desire. Infantile helplessness and the radical disruption in the psyche that results when society suddenly crumbles away – these are traumas the human animal absorbs by forgetting. But forgetting of this kind is never total or final. Repressed memories return as symptoms of inner disorder. They also return as myths.

The necessity of myth follows from Freud's account of the divisions of the human mind. Myths are not eternal archetypes, stored in a cosmic warehouse. In our time, they are fluid, ephemeral and – while being instantly transmissible to millions of people – highly individual.

MYTHS OF THE NEAR FUTURE

Looking out from the hotel balcony shortly after eight o'clock, Kerans watched the sun rise behind the dense groves of giant gymnosperms crowding over the roofs of the abandoned department stores four hundred yards away on the east side of the lagoon. Even through the massive olive-green fronds the relentless power of the sun was plainly tangible. The blunt refracted rays drummed against his bare chest and shoulders, drawing out the first sweat, and he put on a pair of heavy sunglasses to protect his eyes. The solar disc was no longer a well-defined sphere, but a wide expanding ellipse that fanned out across the eastern horizon like a colossal fire-ball, its reflection turning the dead leaden surface of the lagoon into a brilliant copper shield. By noon, less than four hours away, the water would seem to burn.

In these opening lines of J. G. Ballard's *The Drowned World* (1962), Dr Robert Kerans looks out from an upper window of the abandoned Ritz Hotel on a vista of London transformed by climate change.

The bulk of the city had long since vanished, and only the steel-supported buildings of the central commercial and financial areas had survived the encroaching flood waters. The brick houses and single-storey factories of the suburbs had disappeared completely below the drifting tides of silt. Where these broke surface giant forests reared up into the burning dull-green sky, smothering the former wheatfields of temperate Europe and North America. Impenetrable Matto Grossos sometimes three hundred feet high, they were a nightmare world of competing organic forms returning rapidly to their Paleozoic past, and the only avenues of transit for the United Nations military units were through lagoon systems that had superimposed themselves on the former cities. But even these were now being clogged with silt and then submerged.

With the planet returning to a remote geological past, London is being submerged. In the same process Kerans's personal history is disappearing, as pre-human images supplant human memories.

Ballard's was not the first vision of London reverting to swamp. In his novel *After London: Wild England* (1885), the naturalist Richard Jefferies looked to an imagined future in which, after an unspecified catastrophe, the city has been reclaimed by the elements: 'The old men say their fathers told them that soon after the fields were left to themselves a change began to be visible. It became green everywhere in the first spring, after London ended, so that all the country looked alike.' London is submerged by a great lake, and a relapse into barbarism ensues. In time a neo-medieval civilization emerges, more lasting and humane – Jefferies implies – than the civilization that has disappeared. Ballard's vision of London in the aftermath of abrupt climate change is a truer myth. There is no suggestion of any better civilization coming into being, and if the protagonist travels into the past it is not to a pre-modern dream but to a world before the human animal existed.

Recapitulating Ballard's experience as a child in Shanghai – then one of the world's most highly developed cities – the drowned world is unmistakably modern. The descriptions of abandoned hotels, derelict office buildings and drained swimming pools are transmutations of the writer's experiences of Shanghai as it became during the invasion of China by Japanese forces. Ballard spent twenty years forgetting these experiences, he used to say, and another twenty trying to remember them.

For the protagonist of *The Drowned World*, the reversion of the planet to the inhospitable conditions of an earlier geological era is not quite a catastrophe. The effacement of personal memory that the change brings liberates him from an identity that has become burdensome. As his past is wiped away by the memory-erasing landscape, Kerans is able to reconnect with pre-human levels of his own nature. These are not Jung's eternal archetypes, but traces of a planetary past that have been encrypted in his nervous system. Whether these traces are physical structures or images of the protagonist's unconscious devising does not matter: they show the human organism sloughing off personality in a creative response to a life-changing event.

The book ends with Kerans heading into the jungle, leaving scratched on a wall a message he knows no one will read:

27th day. Have rested and am moving south. All is well.
Kerans.

Ballard developed his personal mythology as a response to a trauma in which he discovered that the most seemingly durable features of human life can disappear in a moment. Writing in his memoir *Miracles of Life* (2008) of a cycle ride he took with his father after the Japanese occupation, Ballard recalled stopping off at the Del Monte nightclub and tiptoeing through 'the silent gaming rooms where roulette tables lay on their sides and the floor was covered with broken glasses and betting chips. Gilded statues propped up the canopy of the bars that ran the length of the casino, and on the floor ornate chandeliers cut down from the ceiling tilted among the debris of bottles and old newspapers. Everywhere gold glimmered in the half-light, transforming this derelict casino into a magical cavern from the *Arabian Nights* tales.'

These images contained a message. The empty casino 'held a deeper meaning for me, the sense that reality itself was a stage set that could be dismantled at any moment, and that no matter how magnificent anything appeared, it could be swept aside into the debris of the past'. The ruined gambling club was a cipher for the makeshift of society. 'I also felt that the casino, like the city and the world beyond it, was more real and more meaningful than it had been when it was thronged with gamblers and dancers.' The collapse of Shanghai showed Ballard that everything in human life is provisional and temporary. It also showed him something that is permanent – the inhuman landscape in which humans enact their fates.

The power of myth is in making meaning from the wreckage of meaning. Ballard's mythology turned the dross of childhood trauma into gold; what had been ugly and senseless became something lovely and life-affirming. This transformation took place not in some hermetic process of the sort that Jung dreamt up from his meanderings in medieval alchemy, but in a way that was entirely natural.

Of course the process was not conscious. Myths are not deliberately contrived – or if they are, the result is something like Nietzsche's mythology of the superman, whose power comes by inflating fantasies. True myth is a corrective of fantasy. Think of the story of Icarus, who tried to escape the earth by flying to the heavens on wings of wax, only to fly too close to the sun, which melted the wax and sent him to his death. Or Prometheus, the champion of humankind who stole fire from Zeus, and was punished by being bound to a rock where he had to suffer his liver being eaten by an eagle. These are not stories designed to soothe. The truth they contain has to do with hubris. Icarus and Prometheus deserve to be punished.

Greek myth contains truths that modern myths deny, but not all true myth is ancient. Nowadays myths can be practically momentary: transmitted throughout the world by 24-hour news and the internet, they spread virally, entering the minds of tens and hundreds of millions of people in minutes or hours. Are these true myths, or mass-manufactured fantasies? At times they can be both. In recent years images of resistance to tyranny have been relayed around the world by mass media, many of them captured on mobile phones by the resisters themselves. The myths of revolution that moved the resisters were reinforced, for a time, by the media that make the news. But myths survive for only as long as they are enacted by those who accept them. As popular uprisings go through their normal sequence of rebellion, anarchy and renewed tyranny, the myth of revolution dissipates to be replaced by new myths of conspiracy and betrayal.

Myths are not eternal archetypes frozen some-where out of time. They are more like snatches of music that play in the mind. Seeming to come from nowhere, they stay with us for a while and then are gone.

TLÖN AND HISTORY WITHOUT TWO AFTERNOONS

'I owe the discovery of Uqbar to the conjunction of a mirror and an encyclopedia.' In this opening sentence of Borges's celebrated story 'Tlön, Uqbar, Orbis Tertius', first published in Argentina in 1940, the narrator – a fictive version of Borges – tells us that the discovery of the world of Tlön came about by chance. Following up an interest in an obscure religious sect, the narrator consults the *Anglo-American Cyclopaedia*, 'a literal (though also laggardly) reprint of the *Encyclopaedia Britannica* of 1902', to find out more about the sect and the remote region of Uqbar where it is supposed to have flourished. The *Cyclopaedia* has no entry on Uqbar, but a friend of the narrator brings him another copy of the *Cyclopaedia*, a copy of the same tenth edition of *Britannica*. The second *Cyclopaedia* had four more pages containing an entry on Uqbar, featuring the text, 'For one of those Gnostics, the visible universe was an illusion, or, more precisely, a sophism. Mirrors and fatherhood are hateful because they multiply and proclaim it.' Checking other copies, the narrator finds these pages absent. Later, some months after the death of a friend of his father's, the narrator finds another volume, *A First Encyclopaedia of Tlön*, Vol. XI: Hlaer to Jangr, that had been sent to the friend just days before he died. The book, which had no date or place of publication, produced in the narrator 'a slight, astonished sense of dizziness': 'I now held in my hands a vast and systematic fragment of the history of an unknown planet, with its architectures and its playing cards, the horror of its mythologies and the murmurs of its tongues, its minerals and its birds and fishes, its algebra and its fire, its theological and metaphysical controversies – all joined, coherent, and with no visible doctrinal purpose or hint of parody.'

The discovery leads to an unsuccessful search for other volumes, but the narrator does not doubt that they exist. Described in the missing volumes, the 'brave new world' of Tlön, he conjectures, is 'the work of a secret society of astronomers, biologists, engineers, metaphysicians, poets, chemists, algebrists, moralists, painters, geometers . . . guided and directed by some shadowy man of genius'. 'At first it was thought that Tlön was a mere chaos,' the narrator writes, 'an irresponsible act of imaginative license;

today we know that it is a cosmos, and that the inner-most laws that govern it have been formulated, however provisionally so.'

A feature of Tlön is that its inhabitants are 'con-genitally idealistic'. Everything in their way of thinking presupposes Idealism – the philosophy in which the world is composed not of material objects, existing independently of anyone's perception of them, but of thoughts. Tlön is the world as it was imagined by the Anglo-Irish philosopher George Berkeley (1685–1753), in which the material objects that surround us exist only when they are perceived by us – but without the divine mind, which according to Berkeley keeps these objects in being when they are not perceived by any human observer. In the lan-guage of Tlön there are no nouns, since there are no objects that persist through time, only a succession of acts or events, which 'renders science null' and leaves logic useless.

In a world of this kind philosophy is 'a branch of the literature of fantasy', since 'every philosophy is by definition a dialectical game, a *Philosophie des Als Ob*'. 'The metaphysicians of Tlön seek not truth, or even plausibility – they seek to amaze, astound.' Sys-tems of thought proliferate beyond number, but the philosophers of Tlön are most pleased by those that convey an incongruous semblance of order.

The story concludes with a postscript, supposedly

written in 1947, in which 'the mystery of Tlön' has been 'fully elucidated'. A letter found in 1941 has confirmed the hypothesis that the world of Tlön was invented some time in the early seventeenth century by 'a secret benevolent society', which later included George Berkeley and, in the early nineteenth century, a reclusive American free-thinker and defender of slavery, who first suggested a comprehensive encyclopaedia of the imaginary planet, offering to fund the enterprise provided 'The work shall make no pact with the impostor Jesus Christ.' The free-thinker 'did not believe in God, but wanted to prove to the nonexistent God that mortals could conceive and shape a world'.

By 1914 the work was complete and the 300 members of the secret society had received the last of forty volumes. Another work was planned, even more ambitious, a study of the planet written in one of its languages, to be called *Orbis Tertius*. In 1942, objects from Tlön began to appear. Its blue needle pointing north, a compass was found, the letters on the dial belonging to one of the languages of Tlön. 'This was the first intrusion of the fantastic world of Tlön into the real world.' Some months later, 'small, incredibly heavy cones (made of a metal not of this world)' appeared, which the narrator tells us 'are an image of the deity in certain Tlönian regions'. Other Tlönian objects would follow, undermining the order of the human world.

'Contact with Tlön', the narrator concludes, 'has disintegrated this world.' Humanity is happy for the world to be taken over by Tlön. The intrusion of Tlön – 'a labyrinth forged by men, destined to be deciphered by men' – seemed to show that order can be created by the human mind. 'Almost immediately, reality "caved in" at more than one point. The truth is, it wanted to cave in.' 'Ten years ago' – in the 1930s, towards the end of which Borges conceived and wrote the story – 'any symmetry, any system with an appearance of order – dialectical materialism, anti-Semitism, Nazism – could spellbind and hypnotize mankind. How could the world not fall under the spell of Tlön, how could it not yield to the vast and minutely detailed evidence of an ordered planet?'

A symbol of the human dream of order, Tlön first offers an escape from chaos and then – like Christianity and its humanist successors – creates even more disorder. Religious and secular believers say this chaos comes from the misuse of their faith by sinful or fallible human beings. If importing Tlön does not bring order into human life, it is because humans are not yet fit to live in Tlön. But Tlön appears orderly only in the pages of the *Encyclopaedia* – a human artifice. In reality – the fictive reality of Tlön – the world is chaotic. Borges tells us as much, when he describes Tlön as being composed of a series of discrete events, irreducibly different and unconnected with one another either by cause and effect or by logic. Tlön cannot avoid reproducing the frailty of reason. Not only are the hidden workings of the mind ignorant of logic, as Freud pointed out. Logic itself is a fictional construction: any system of ideas that aims to be clear and self-consistent breaks down in ambiguities and contradictions. Tlön is not chaotic by chance. The chaos of Tlön is, in fact, the chaos of the human mind.

Is it possible to imagine a world in which humans were not possessed by a fiction of order – a world which for that very reason might be less of a chaos? Borges poses the question in a poem, 'Things that Might Have Been':

> I think of things that might have been and
>   never were.
> The treatise on Saxon myths that Bede omitted
>   to write.
> The inconceivable work that Dante may have
>   glimpsed
> As soon as he corrected the Comedy's last
>   verse.
> History without two afternoons: that of the
>   hemlock, that of the Cross.

Borges identifies two fictions that have shaped history in the west: Jesus on the cross and Socrates taking the hemlock. Seemingly at odds, these two deaths convey the same assurance. Jesus is an incarnation of God, an eternal Being, while Socrates (as represented by Plato) has access to a realm of eternal forms. Their lives are examples of *Logos* – a principle of order – at work in history.

It is true that, without those two afternoons, history would surely have been different. But life would still be ruled by fictions. Finding themselves in a world they do not understand human beings will always create imaginary worlds, which like Tlön will also be unintelligible.

WORDS AND CINDERS

'There is a difficulty in finding a comprehensive scheme of the cosmos, because there is none. The cosmos is only *organised* in parts; the rest is cinders.' The author of this observation, the poet T. E. Hulme, published only six poems in his lifetime. In the decade before he was killed in the trenches at Flanders in 1917, he produced a stream of provocative writings on philosophy and language, defending a radical version of nominalism – the philosophy according to which only individual things exist, which language bundles together for practical purposes – against the rival philosophy of realism, which holds that abstract ideas reflect natural kinds of things.

The difference between nominalism and realism is

not a dusty dispute among philosophers. It expresses diverging turns of mind, which view the human world in very different ways. Many people think the world is like a book. The pages may be torn and the print smudged; we may find some pages missing, or forget the book in a taxi. But if only we could read the text in full, we would understand the world in which we find ourselves.

Hulme thought differently. In a series of notes he began in 1906–7, which he called 'Cinders', he wrote: 'Never think in a book: here are Truth and all the other capital letters; but think in a theatre and watch the audience. Here is the reality, here are human animals. Listen to the words of heroism and then look at the crowded husbands who applaud. All philosophies are subordinate to this. It is not a question of the unity of the world and men afterwards put into it, *but* of human animals, and of philosophies as an elaboration of their appetites.'

Human beings are animals that have equipped themselves with symbols. Helping deal with a world they do not understand, symbols are useful tools; but humans have an inveterate tendency to think and act as if the world they have made from these symbols actually exists. Their minds – they like to think – are built on the model of the cosmos. A great deal of philosophy and religion is not much more than a rationalization of this conceit.

Hulme proposed another view: 'The truth is that there are no ultimate principles, upon which the whole of knowledge can be built once and for ever as on a rock. But there are an infinity of analogues, which help us along, and give us a feeling of power over the chaos when we perceive them. The field is infinite and herein lies the chance for originality. Here there are some new things under the sun.'

The human animal is not an imperfect embodiment of some higher order in things, existing apart from the world or slowly evolving within it. 'Man is the chaos highly organised, but liable to revert to chaos at any moment.' The world is not a harmony we dimly perceive. 'The eyes, the beauty of the world, have been organised out of the faeces. Man returns to dust. So does the face of the world to primeval cinders.' Moralists and logicians tell us their laws are not just human conventions – they describe something independent of human beings, something more absolute. For Hulme, however, 'The *absolute* is not to be described as perfect, but if existent as essentially imperfect, chaotic and cinder-like. (Even this view is not ultimate, but merely designed to satisfy temporary human analogies and wants.)' People talk of humans evolving, as if the views of the world humans take up and leave behind are developing towards one that will be all inclusive. But worldviews are like gardens, easily destroyed by bad weather. 'The unity of Nature is an extremely artificial and fragile bridge, a garden net.' Human ideas are temporary clearances in the waste. 'Certain groups of ideas as huts for men to live in.' Most of the time, the cindery realities go unseen. But they never go away. Civilization is built on an ash-heap. 'In an organised city it is not easy to see the cinder element of earth – all is banished. But it is easy to see it psychologically. What the Nominalists call the grit in the machine, I call the fundamental element of the machine.'

Hulme's view of the human animal he calls classical and contrasts with another he calls Romantic. In the Romantic view humans are only by accident limited creatures: their possibilities are infinite. In a classical view, humans are essentially finite; human potential is fixed and narrow. 'Put shortly, these are the two views. One, that man is intrinsically good, spoilt by circumstance; and the other that he is intrinsically limited, but disciplined by order and tradition to something fairly decent . . . The view which regards man as a well, a reservoir full of possibilities, I call the romantic; the one which regards him as a very finite and fixed creature, I call the classical.'

Each of the two views comes in a number of versions. What Hulme describes as the classical view might seem opposed to religion, at least where religion involves the idea that humans partake of divinity. But where religion has recognized human imperfectibility – as in the Christian idea of original sin – religion expresses the classical view. Hulme sees Romanticism as a religious impulse: 'By the perverted logic of Rationalism, your natural instincts are repressed . . . The instincts that find their right and proper outlet in religion come out in some other way. You don't believe in a God, so you begin to believe that man is a god. You don't believe in heaven, so you begin to believe in a heaven on earth. In other words, you get romanticism . . . Romanticism then, and this is the best definition I can give of it, is spilt religion.'

But the idea that human possibilities are unbounded has also been promoted by rationalists, including enthusiasts for science who think the growth of knowledge enables the human animal to overcome the limits of the natural world. So it is not only in Romanticism that a view of humans as being able to transcend their nature has spilled over from Christianity. By the logic of Hulme's argument – and this is true as a matter of fact – rationalism is also spilt religion.

Hulme was one of the founders of the Imagist current in early twentieth-century poetry, which included poets such as Ford Madox Ford, Ezra Pound, F. S. Flint and 'H.D.' (Hilda Doolittle) and influenced later poets such as D. H. Lawrence and William Carlos

Williams. The Imagists aimed for a certain sort of exactness – not a factually accurate description of an object, but a precise rendition of particular impressions. As they saw it, ordinary language is a succession of compromises perpetuated by habit. As Hulme put it:

> The great aim is accurate, precise and definite description. The first thing is to recognise how extraordinarily difficult this is. It is no mere matter of carefulness: you have to use language, and language is by its very nature a communal thing; that is, it expresses never the exact thing but a compromise – that which is common to you, me and everybody. But each man sees a little differently, and to get out clearly and exactly what he does see, he must have a terrific struggle with language, whether it be with words or the technique of other arts. Language has its own special nature, its own conventions and communal ideas. It is only by a concentrated effort of mind that you can hold it fixed to your own purpose.

The result of the struggle with language would be a type of 'hard, dry, classical verse', which would render sensation in a fresh way. What he had in mind might be illustrated by his poem 'Autumn':

A touch of cold in the Autumn night
I walked abroad,
And saw the ruddy moon lean over a hedge
Like a red-faced farmer.
I did not stop, but nodded;
And round about were the wistful stars
With white faces like town children.

The Imagist approach to language led to a revolution in poetry. But seeing things as the Imagists did meant more than a change in the technique of verse. For Hulme it meant an attitude to the world, which included a readiness to risk his own life when what he viewed as high values were at stake. When the Great War broke out in August 1914 he joined the army as a private soldier. His experiences in the trenches confirmed his view that the world is chaotic: 'It's curious to think of the ground between the trenches, a bank which is practically never seen by anyone in the daylight, as it is only safe to move through it at dark. It's full of dead things, dead animals here and there, dead unburied animals, skeletons of horses destroyed by shell fire. It's curious to think of it later on in the war, when it will again be seen in daylight.'

Hulme was wounded and while convalescing in England published under the name of 'North Staffs' a series of polemical essays in support of the war. His main target of attack was Bertrand Russell, an opponent of the war who was at the time close to pacifism. Hulme's arguments appealed to the need for values other than those recognized in a rationalist, utilitarian ethic: while he had no sympathy for jingoism, he insisted on the need for 'a more heroic or tragic system of ethical values' – values that are 'above life'. Consistently with his anti-rationalist philosophy, Hulme accepted that these arguments could not justify the conflict that was under way. 'All I urge against Mr Russell's ethical premises might be entirely true, and yet, at the same time, this war might be the most colossal stupidity in history.'

Hulme's afterthought was premonitory. Taking up a commission in the Royal Marines Artillery in March 1916, he returned to the trenches where he was killed by a shell burst in September 1917. As a result of the war civilization in Europe – which he believed he was in some way defending – descended into a kind of barbarism that he could not have imagined.

GODLESS MYSTICISM

I shall attempt again to say the unsayable, to express with poor words what I have to give

devout infidels in nominalistic mysticism, in sceptical mysticism . . . The world does not exist twice.
There is no God apart from the world, nor a
world apart from God. This conviction has been
called pantheism . . . Why not? They are after all
but words. In the highest mystical ecstasy the Ego
experiences that it has become God. Why not?
Shall I quarrel about words? For a decade I have
been teaching: the feeling of the Ego is a delusion
. . . Are these mere philosophical word-sequences?
Games of language? No. What I can experience is
no longer mere language. And I can experience,
for short hours, that I no longer know anything
about the principle of individuation, that there
ceases to be a difference between the world and
myself.

The author of this passage, the prolific writer-
philosopher Fritz Mauthner (1849–1923), is nowadays remembered chiefly for a remark directed
against him in Wittgenstein's *Tractatus Logico-
Philosophicus*: 'All philosophy is a "critique of
language" (though not in Mauthner's sense).' Partly
as a result of this dismissal, Mauthner had practically
no influence on philosophy in the twentieth century.
Like his near-contemporary, Mauthner – born in a
small town in Bohemia and growing up in Prague

speaking Czech, German and Hebrew – was a product of the subtle and brilliant intellectual culture of the late Habsburg empire, and much of Wittgenstein's hugely influential philosophy used ideas borrowed from him. When Wittgenstein compared the critique of language to climbing a ladder and then throwing it away and wrote of language as being like an ancient city or a game, he was echoing formulations that occur in the first thirty pages of Mauthner's three-volume *Contributions to a Critique of Language* (Stuttgart, 1901–3; second edition, 1923). Yet Mauthner's writings are invigoratingly different from the type of philosophy that Wittgenstein's work spawned. In many ways Wittgenstein stands at the opposite pole from the forgotten predecessor from whom he took so much.

Neglected by philosophers, Mauthner's inquiries into language had a more fruitful impact on literature. Samuel Beckett – the twentieth-century writer most devoted to taking language to its limits – read Mauthner's *Critique* some time towards the end of the 1930s, making copious notes (some of which he would read to James Joyce), and still had Mauthner's three-volume book on his shelf forty years later. Confirming the influence of Mauthner's critique on his writings, Beckett wrote in a letter in 1978:

For me it came down to:

> Thought words
> Words inane
> Thought inane
> Such was my levity.

Beckett expanded on this in an entry in a diary he kept around the time he first read Mauthner:

> we feel with terrible resignation that reason is not a superhuman gift bestowed on humanity, that it is not an unchanging and eternal deity, that reason evolved in humanity and evolved into what it is, but that it also, however, could have evolved differently . . . what we hold to be the eternal and unalterably fixed laws of our intellectual being [are] merely a game played by the coincidence that is the world; when we recognise that our reason (which, after all, is language) can only be a coincidental reason, then we will only smile when we consider the argumentative passion with which anthropologists have laboured over questions of custom, belief and collective psychological 'facts'.

The impact of Mauthner's work may be clearest in the novel *Watt*, written while Beckett was a member of the French Resistance on the run from the Gestapo and published in 1953, in which the difficulties of communication and the impossibility of knowledge are central themes. But Mauthner's doubts about language can be heard throughout Beckett's work. The last sentence of Mauthner's book reads, 'Pure critique is but an articulated laughter.' Beckett's life-long struggle with language eventuated in laughter – the gibes and guffaws of his drama and the lapidary humour of his later prose – and then in 'the silence that underlies All'.

Like Mauthner's, Beckett's writings are attempts to say the unsayable. As he put it in a letter that echoes Mauthner: 'On the way to this literature of the unword, which is so desirable to me, some form of Nominalist irony might be a necessary stage.' Becoming silent meant stilling the internal monologue that is the dubious privilege of human self-awareness, a task that involved countless experiments with language. Since human beings cannot live in silence this wilful wordplay was a kind of folly, as Beckett recognized in the last text he ever wrote, an unfinished work he produced months before he died in a nursing home:

> folly –
> folly for to –
> for two –

folly from this –
all this . . .
what is the word –
what is the word

If Beckett's work aimed for silence, it was not because he supposed that silence would bring peace. As Mauthner wrote:

The need for peace seduces the human mind into seeing the mirage of a resting-place in the desert of its striving for knowledge; the scholars believe in their linguistic roots. At all times and in all places, the science of a particular time is the expression of the poor human spirit's wistful desire for rest. Only critique – wherever it is still alive in even poorer heads – may not rest, for it cannot rest. It must rudely awaken science, remove its illusion of an oasis, and drive it further along on the hot, deadly, and possibly aimless desert paths.

Wittgenstein's goal was a resting-place of the sort Mauthner describes. Even in the *Tractatus*, Wittgenstein seemed to be looking to philosophy as a therapy that would release him from doubt. In his later work he campaigned incessantly against scepticism, not by developing an alternative philosophical position – the later Wittgenstein claimed to have no such positions – but by claiming that sceptical questioning resulted from mistaken ways of thinking about words. Ordinary language was a form of life that needed – and permitted – nothing beyond itself. Humans were figures in a world they had themselves made. Peace – the peace that Wittgenstein fantasized he would enjoy when he could give up philosophy – meant accepting that this human world is all that there ever can be.

Mauthner's work also had a therapeutic goal, but not that of finding peace by stilling doubt. Like Hulme and Beckett a radical nominalist, Mauthner wanted to loosen the hold of words on the mind. Rather than struggling to silence the impulse to move beyond words, he wanted to follow the impulse wherever it led. His writings on mysticism show where that led him. An uncompromising atheist and author of a four-volume history of atheist thinking, Mauthner noted that 'atheism' – like 'God' – is only a word. His atheism has nothing in common with the evangelical unbelief of his day or ours. In a pure form, atheism is no more to do with unbelief than religion is about belief. Strictly understood, atheism is an entirely negative position. You are not an atheist if you deny what theists affirm. You are an atheist if you have no use for the concepts and doctrines of theism.

Atheism of this rigorous kind has something in

common with negative theology, which denies that God can be captured in ideas or beliefs. Mauthner admired Meister Eckhart, a fourteenth-century Christian mystic who died in obscure circumstances after being subjected to trial by the Inquisition, as a true atheist, since Eckhart insisted that nothing could be said of God – not even that God existed.

Negative theologians use language as Mauthner thought it should be used: to point to something (not a thing in any ordinary sense) that cannot be expressed in words. If only that is real which can be captured in language, God is unreal. But it is not only 'God' that is unreal in this way. So are all general terms including 'matter' and 'humanity' – abstractions that have featured in the catechisms of unbelief. Atheism does not mean rejecting 'belief in God'. It means giving up belief in language as anything other than a practical convenience. The world is not a creation of language, but something that – like the God of the negative theologians – escapes language. Atheism is only a stage on the way to a more far-reaching scepticism.

Mauthner called this view – 'just in order to have a word-symbol' – godless mysticism. What he was trying to articulate could not be expressed in language. That did not mean there was nothing to express. In the *Tractatus* (7.7), Wittgenstein famously declared, 'Whereof one cannot speak, thereof one must be silent.' Given the view of language he later developed, there was nothing for Wittgenstein to be silent about. For Mauthner, on the other hand, what could not be spoken was more important than anything that could be put into words.

Godless mystics do not look to merge themselves with something larger they have imagined into being; they look to wipe away their inexistent selves. In John Ashbery's words:

> The sands are frantic
> In the hourglass. But there is time
> To change, to utterly destroy
> That too-familiar image
> Lurking in the glass
> Each morning, at the edge of the mirror.

3 Another Sunlight

The prevalence of those gray flakes falling?
They are sun motes. You have slept in the sun
Longer than the sphinx, and are none the wiser
for it.

John Ashbery

THE LIGHT-DRENCHED PRISM

'The air is cool, embalmed with hay and flowers.
Blackbirds and thrushes sing. The hobby flies stead-
ily towards the distant wood, carrying a dark and
broken swift in its talons. This is now a different
place from what it was two hours ago. There is no
mysterious essence we can call a "place". Place is
change. Its motion is killed by the mind, and pre-
served in the amber of memory.' This thought on
the nature of place came to someone who spent a

decade of his life watching birds in a small patch of Essex. In *The Peregrine*, J. A. Baker recorded his pursuit of the peregrine falcon. 'For ten years I followed the peregrine. I was possessed. It was a grail to me.' Baker was not a birdwatcher in the usual sense of the term, though he came to know a good deal about the ways of birds. Nor was he a hunter, though he wrote of joining the peregrine in its hunting. 'Wherever he goes, this winter, I will follow him. I will share the fear, and the exaltation, and the boredom, of the hunting life. I will follow him till my predatory human shape no longer darkens in terror the shaken kaleidoscope of colour that stains the deep fovea of his brilliant eye. My pagan heart shall sink into the winter land, and there be purified.'

The book that Baker wrote – where he condensed the ten years into a single winter – has been read as a piece of nature writing. But it is quite different from most books of this genre, which aim to show what people can gain from observing the natural world. Baker's goal was more radical. *The Peregrine* is a tribute to the sense of freedom the bird evoked in Baker as he watched it in flight; but, more than that, the book is a record of the author's struggle to see the landscape in which he pursued the bird through the eyes of the bird itself. He followed the peregrine not in order to observe it, but in an attempt to escape the point of view of a human observer.

At times Baker felt as if he had shed his human identity and become the bird:

> . . . I shut my eyes and tried to crystallise my will into the light-drenched prism of the hawk's mind. Warm and firm-footed in the long grass smelling of the sun, I sank into the skin and blood and bones of the hawk. The ground became a branch to my feet, the sun on my eyelids was heavy and warm. Like the hawk, I heard and hated the sound of man . . . I felt the pull of the north, the mystery and fascination of the migrating gulls. I shared the same strange yearning to be gone. I sank down and slept the feather-light sleep of the hawk. Then I woke him with my waking.

Hunting the hawk, Baker lost sight of himself.

> My eyes turned quickly about, alert for the walking heads of men. Unconsciously I was imitating the movements of a hawk, as in some primitive ritual: the hunter becoming the thing he hunts. I looked into the wood. In a lair of shadow the peregrine was crouching, watching me, gripping the neck of a dead branch. We live, in these days in the open, the same ecstatic fearful life. We shun men.

We hate their suddenly uplifted arms, the insanity of their flailing gestures, their erratic scissoring gait, their aimless stumbling ways, the tombstone whiteness of their faces.

In the only other book he wrote, *The Hill of Summer*, Baker reports a similar shift of identity with a fox:

I came to a sunlit clearing barred with long shadows . . . The bracken swished, and separated, and a fox suddenly appeared in the narrow path ahead of me. My smell must have been far more pungent than his glandular stench was to me, but for a long time he did nothing. He had been moving very slowly, as though pondering, perhaps not yet fully awake after his daylight sleep. Watching his pale yellow and white face, slightly darker in colour about the amber shining eyes, I seemed to feel the soft mask of the fox pass over me. I felt the fetid breath, the questing nose that never sleeps, the hot cloak of senses so keen as to be unbearable to man. I stifled in the mask of the fox, as though I was his earth, his refuge. Then this strange feeling faded; and there was the fox again, a yard in front of me. Without any sign that he recognised me as an enemy, he walked slowly past and vanished into the bracken.

Aside from farmers and hunters, whose sounds he hears in the distance, Baker is the sole human being to feature in his two books, and he appears rarely. From the little that can be known, his outward life seems to have been uneventful. The son of a draughts-man who worked in a local engineering company, he lived all of it (1926–87) in Chelmsford, leaving school at sixteen and never going to university. From letters he wrote to a friend, it is known that he worked in a variety of jobs, mostly casual, including a few months pushing trolleys in the British Museum. Eventually he became manager of the local Automobile Association, then manager of a depot of the Britvic soft-drinks company. Despite working for the AA, he never learnt to drive. His birdwatching was conducted by cycling in the countryside surrounding Chelmsford. His pursuit of the peregrine, some parts of which are described in diaries published in his *Complete Works*, stretched from the mid-1950s to the mid-1960s. By the time he published *The Hill of Summer* he was becoming disabled as a result of rheumatoid arthritis, but he continued to birdwatch with the help of his wife Doreen (to whom he was married for thirty-one years and to whom he dedicated *The Peregrine*), who drove him out to the country where he could sit and walk and be taken back in the evening. He died of cancer, a side-effect of the treatment he was receiving for the arthritis.

When Baker was watching the peregrine, the land-scape around Chelmsford showed itself to him in a different light. 'I have tried to convey the beauty of this bird and to convey the wonder of the land he lived in, a land as profuse and glorious to me as Africa.' A shift of perspective revealed another country.

> Looking down, the hawk saw the big orchard beneath him shrink into dark twiggy lines and green strips; saw the dark woods closing together and reaching out across the hills; saw the green and white fields turning to brown; saw the silver line of the brook, and the coiled river slowly uncoiling; saw the whole valley flattening and wid-ening; saw the horizon staining with distant towns; saw the estuary lifting up its blue and silver mouth, tongued with green islands. And beyond, beyond all, he saw the straight-ruled line of the sea floating like a rim of mercury on the surface of the brown and white land. The sea, easing as he rose, lifted its blazing storm of light, and thundered freedom to the land-locked hawk.

The countryside Baker knew – 'dim, flat, desolate lands that cauterise all sorrow' – became a new coun-try. 'Like the seafarer, the peregrine lives in a pouring-away world of no attachment, a world of wakes and tilting, of sinking planes of land and water. We who are anchored and earth-bound cannot envisage this freedom of the eye.'

'The hardest thing of all', Baker wrote, 'is to see what is really there.' The places he saw shifted and vanished with changes in the light. 'The spirit of this place is elusive, it escapes into the surrounding air. Yet something breathes upon the edge of vision, like rain beginning. It touches the senses lightly, then departs. At a distance the grove seems to have entity, the self-possession of a single tree. But go in, and at once the wholeness leaps apart, fragmenting into more than individual trees.' Light does not pass over unchanging places. Moving across an unknown landscape, it creates the places that the eye sees. 'Cold air rises from the ground as the sun goes down. The eye-burning clarity of the light intensifies. The southern rim of the sky glows to a deeper blue, to pale violet, to purple, then thins to grey. Slowly the wind falls, and the still air begins to freeze . . . The long, cold amber of the afterglow casts clear black lunar shadows. There is an animal mystery in the light that sets upon the fields like a frozen muscle that will flex and wake at sunrise.'

Baker did not aim to render what he saw in any literal way. 'Cotswold is its own place, withdrawn, remote. It has its own light, and cold, and sky, and monarchy of cloud. It will not be meshed in words.'

The landscape seemed to come from a primordial past. 'It was the clearest, coldest day I have ever known . . . a heron stood deep in the snow. The gale did not rock him; his long grey feathers were unruffled. Regal and frozen and dead, he stood to the wind in his thin sarcophagus of ice. Already he seemed to be dynasties away from me. I have outlived him, as the gibbering ape outlived the dinosaur.'

The hawk was Baker's point of exit from the human world. 'I have always longed to be a part of the outward life, to be out there at the edge of things, to let the human taint wash away in emptiness and silence as the fox sloughs his smell into the cold unworldliness of water; to return to the town as a stranger.' Returning to the town, he was surprised by beauty. Seen through a hawk's eyes the works of humans had the look of natural things. 'To hawks, these gritty country lanes must look like shingle beaches; the polished roads must gleam like seams of granite in a moorland waste. All the monstrous artefacts of man are natural, untainted things to them.'

Baker knew that there was in fact no way out of the human world. Becoming for a short time a stranger to himself, he did not cease to be human. He could visit the new places that were created by light. He could not leave the human ruins. 'Walls of red brick, mellowed by golden lichen, enclose a forgotten garden, the hush of an empty house. The white blossom of a pear tree clouds above the wall, burning white on the blue of the sky. Bullfinches call within, softly, made distant and exotic by the pored redness of the wall. I can imagine the cock-bird's breast, brick-red, clean and softly pure. This seems to be the heart of the wood. The light is deeper here, and there is a feeling of imminent revelation. But it is illusory.'

He knew the natural world was no haven of peace. 'I shall try to make clear the bloodiness of killing. Too often this has been slurred over by those who defend hawks. Flesh-eating man is in no way superior. It is so easy to love the dead. The word "predator" is baggy with misuse. All birds eat living flesh at some time in their lives. Consider the cold-eyed thrush, the springy carnivore of lawns, worm stabber, basher to death of snails. We should not sentimentalise his song, and forget the killing that sustains it.' He knew how much suffering is hidden by beauty. 'So much cruelty is mercifully concealed from us by the sheltering leaves. We seldom see the bones of pain that hang beyond the green summer day. The woods and fields and gardens are places of endless stabbing, impaling, squashing and mangling. We see only what floats to the surface: the colour, the song, the nesting, and the feeding. I do not think we could bear a clear vision of the animal world.' Walking in the woods and seeing a bullfinch biting off a bud from a twig, he cannot help thinking of the violence of bird life: 'the pull and twist of his bill to break off a bud reminded me of a peregrine breaking the neck of its prey. Whatever is destroyed, the act of destruction does not vary very much. Beauty is vapour from the pit of death.'

The hawk's view of the land was the work of Baker's imagination. The horror from which he was fleeing was a world in which humans encountered only reflections of themselves. If he could not exit from this world, he did step close to the edge of human vision. Without looking at things through a bird's eyes, he peeled away enough of himself to be able to look out through eyes that were no longer those he had had before. Spending so many days, over so many years, in a narrow strip of land, he came to see places as momentary events, not enduring things. 'Hawk-hunting sharpens vision. Pouring away behind the moving bird, the land flows out from the eye in deltas of piercing colour. The angled eye strikes through the surface dross as the oblique axe cuts to the heart of the tree. A vivid sense of place grows like another limb.' It was not only place that was changed. For Baker – perhaps aware, in his later years of following the peregrine, that his illness was making the sand in the hourglass flow more quickly – time passed differently. 'Time is measured by a clock of blood . . . the memory of a certain fulmination or declension of light that was unique to that time and that place on that day, a memory as vivid to the hunter as burning magnesium.'

'Another sunlight', writes Stevens, 'might make another world.' There are as many worlds as there are shifts in the light. We are too much shut in ourselves to notice these vanishing places. Monks and mystics try to still the mind so that it can grasp what is eternal. Baker did the opposite, sharpening his senses so he could catch up with things that came and went in a flash. 'I came late to the love of birds. For years I saw them only as a tremor at the edge of vision. They know suffering and joy in simple states not possible for us. Their lives quicken and warm to a pulse our hearts can never reach. They race to oblivion.'

People who love other creatures are often accused of anthropomorphizing them. This was not true of Baker. Rather than anthropomorphizing other species, Baker tried the experiment of deanthropomorphizing himself. Seeing the world as he imagined hawks might see it, he was able at times to be something other than he had been. He too raced to oblivion, losing himself as he followed the peregrine.

THE SILENCE OF ANIMALS

The pursuit of silence seems to be a peculiarly human activity. Other animals run away from noise, but it is noise made by others that they try to avoid. Only humans want to silence the clamour in their minds.

Tiring of the inner chatter, they turn to silence in order to deafen the sound of their thoughts. What people are seeking when they look for silence is a different kind of noise.

Human institutions that are set up to cultivate silence are full of this noise. It is only when they are empty that churches are silent – and often not even then. The droning prayers leave a never-ending din, the dull echo of the human anecdote being monotonously rehearsed. This clamour falls away in churches that are derelict, particularly when they have been deserted for a long time. A church that has been worn away by the elements contains a silence not found in one that still contains worshippers.

Writing in the Introduction to *A Time to Keep Silence*, an account of retreats he took in French monasteries in the 1950s, the author, soldier and traveller Patrick Leigh Fermor laments the dereliction into which many of these institutions have fallen:

They emerge in the fields like the peaks of a vanished Atlantis drowned four centuries deep. The gutted cloisters stand uselessly among the furrows and only broken pillars mark the former symmetry of the aisles and ambulatories. Surrounded by elder-flower, with their bases tangled in bracken and broken spandrels that fly spinning over the tree tops in slender trajectories, the clustering pil-

lars suspend the great empty circumference of a
rose window in the rook-haunted sky. It is as
though some tremendous Gregorian chant had
been interrupted hundreds of years ago to hang
there petrified in its climax ever since.

Leigh Fermor might not seem the type to be in
need of silence. Devoting much of his life to pleasure and adventure, a renowned bon viveur and
conversationalist, he walked across Europe in 1933
at the age of eighteen, an experience that, much later
– for he was also a perfectionist – produced two
travel books of extraordinary vividness and style, *A
Time of Gifts* (1977) and *Between the Woods and
the Water* (1986). Serving in the Special Operations
Executive in the Second World War, he lived in the
mountains of Crete for two years disguised as a
shepherd and led the party that kidnapped the
German commander of the island – an episode portrayed in the film *Ill Met by Moonlight* (1950).
Living a long life – he died in 2011 at the age of
ninety-six – he remained active until the end, swimming in the Aegean in his late eighties and eating a
good dinner the day before he died.

The idea that a human being of this sort cannot
yearn for silence is a prejudice rather than a well-
founded fact. Action may be fated, but the urgency
of life does not remove the need for contemplation.

Facing a world war in which everything he valued of civilization might be extinguished, Leigh Fermor had no choice but to fight. He could no more stand aside from the conflict than could Arthur Koestler. But action is not the whole of life or always life's most valuable part, and it is often the most active individuals who most need the release of contemplation. It is only the inordinate self-regard of modern people that leads them to suppose that the most venturesome human beings can be satisfied with human company.

While he might have agreed that the desolate remains of former monasteries have a silence not found in working houses of the spirit, Leigh Fermor regretted the decline of monastic life. He was right to do so. Churches and monasteries show that silence is not the normal human condition. Silencing themselves – and, even more, others – comes naturally to humans, but not being silent. That is why humans are impelled to seek silence. The abbeys and convents that spanned Europe in pre-modern times, and the vast rookeries of monks and nuns that existed in Tibet until they were destroyed in the late twentieth century, were not mere survivals of feudalism. They testified to a need that is quintessentially human, which modern societies repress but which has not ceased to demand satisfaction.

If silence is no longer cultivated, it is because admitting the need for it means accepting that you are inwardly restless – a condition, in other times recognized as one of misery, that is now prized as a virtue. 'I have often said', writes Pascal, 'that the sole cause of man's unhappiness is that he does not know how to stay quietly in his room.' If you admit your need for silence, you accept that much of your life has been an exercise in distraction. 'Men who are naturally conscious of what they are shun nothing as much as rest; they would do anything to be disturbed.'

When you think of life as a state of constant unrest, you want to be disturbed all the time. Work fends off the heavier burden of idleness, and even the round of commuting helps muffle the inner murmuring. That being constantly occupied is a form of distraction has long been known. It is only lately that the pursuit of distraction has been embraced as the meaning of life.

Going in search of silence means accepting that the life of action is not enough, a fact few people will today admit. Old-fashioned religious practitioners, who accept that fulfilment cannot be found in the world, are more realistic. But the religious have their own diversions, and among these is the idea that the need for silence is a mark of the superiority of humans over other animals. In *The World of Silence*, the Swiss Catholic theologian Max Picard writes:

The silence of animals is different from the silence of men. The silence of men is transparent and bright because it confronts the world, releasing the word in every moment and receiving it back into itself again . . . Animals have a heavy silence. Like a block of stone. Animals stride over the blocks of silence, trying to tear themselves away but always chained to them.

Silence is isolated in animals; therefore they are lonely.

It is as though the silence in animals was materially tangible. It makes its way right through the outside of the animal, and animals are unredeemed not only because they lack speech, but because the silence itself is unredeemed: it is a hard, coagulated silence.

While it is true that the quality of silence is different in other animals, the difference is not that of which Picard writes. Whereas silence is for other animals a natural state of rest, for humans silence is an escape from inner commotion. By nature volatile and discordant, the human animal looks to silence for relief from being itself while other creatures enjoy silence as their birthright. Humans seek silence because they seek redemption from themselves, other animals live in silence because they do not need redeeming.

Picard's inversion of the qualities of animal and human silence puts humans on a pedestal in much the same way as does Martin Heidegger's claim that other animals are 'world-poor'. In Heidegger's neo-Christian view rats and tigers, gorillas and hyenas simply exist, reacting passively to the world around them. Lacking any perception of the mysterious 'Being' from whence they came, other animals are no more than objects. Humans, on the other hand, are not objects, since they shape the world in which they live.

This dreary old story is best forgotten. Every sentient creature is a world-maker. The floating world of the hawk is as much a creation of the hawk as our landlocked world is of humans. There may be a sense in which other animals are poor, but their poverty is an ideal that humans will never attain. When Christians and their humanist followers disparage the silence of animals, it may be envy that moves them.

The distance between human and animal silence is a consequence of the use of language. It is not that other creatures lack language. The discourse of the birds is more than a human metaphor. Cats and dogs stir in their sleep, and talk to themselves as they go about their business. Only humans use words to construct a self-image and a story of their lives. But if other animals lack this interior monologue, it is not clear why this should put humans on a higher plane. Why should breaking silence and then loudly struggling to renew it be such an achievement?

Many people think humans are unique in possessing something called consciousness. At its most refined, thinking in this way is like thinking that the universe has come up with humans so that it can look at itself:

> We come from nothing and return to it.
> It lends us out to time, and when we lie
> In silent contemplation of the void
> They say we feel it contemplating us.
> This is wrong, but who could bear the truth.
> We are ourselves the void in contemplation.
> We are its only nerve and hand and eye.

Humans are the void looking at itself. It is a lovely image. But why privilege humans in this way? The eyes of other creatures may be brighter. Humans cannot help seeing the world through the veil of language. When they run after silence they are trying to leave behind the signs that make their world. This struggle is as universally human as language itself. Through poetry, religion and immersion in the natural world, humans try to shed the words that enshroud their lives. At bottom, that is what they are doing when they struggle to be silent. The struggle can never succeed, but that does not make it pointless.

Philosophers will say that humans can never be silent because the mind is made of words. For these half-witted logicians, silence is no more than a word. To overcome language by means of language is obviously impossible. Turning within, you will find only words and images that are parts of yourself. But if you turn outside yourself – to the birds and animals and the quickly changing places where they live – you may hear something beyond words. Even humans can find silence, if they can bring themselves to forget the silence they are looking for.

A VISIT TO THE BRITISH MUSEUM

For the human visitor the British Museum may seem like a depository of obsolete gods. Among the varied artefacts that it contains none produces a more intense sense of transiency than the images of worship that are collected there. The domed building houses many objects that were used in ways of life that have long since ceased to exist, but the images of gods have the added poignancy of being made in reverence to deities that were themselves imagined to be eternal. Among those who made these images, there can be few who perceived that the gods were themselves human artefacts. If they had realized that the deities whose images they were leaving behind were figments, what might they have felt?

Written some time in 1929–30, William Empson's 'Homage to the British Museum' is a meditation on the evanescence of the gods:

> Attending there let us absorb the cultures of
>   nations
> And dissolve into our judgement all their codes.
> Then, being clogged with a natural hesitation
> (People are continually asking one the way out)
> Let us stand here and admit we have no road.
> Being everything, let us admit that is to be
>   something,
> Or give ourselves the benefit of the doubt.
> Let us offer our pinch of dust all to this God,
> And grant his reign over the entire building.

Empson's tranquil acceptance that gods are as mortal as the ways of life they sanctify is rare in modern times. For those that cannot bear to live without belief, any faith is better than none. This is the appeal of fundamentalism, which promises to banish the lack of meaning by an act of will. Hence, also, the god-building enthusiasm of humanists, who announce the arrival of a new deity, uglier than any that has ever before been worshipped, a divinized version of themselves . . .

In 'The Pigeons at the British Museum' (1884), Richard Jefferies described the Museum's pigeons as visitors who saw the building as a feature of the natural world:

To them the building is merely a rock, pierced with convenient caverns; they use its exterior for their purpose, but penetrate no further. With air and light, the sunlit gravel, the green lawn between it and the outer railings – with these they are concerned, and with these only. The heavy roll of the traffic in Oxford Street, audible here, is nothing to them; the struggle for money does not touch them, they let it go by. Nor the many minds searching and re-searching in the great Library, this mental toil is no more to them than the lading of the wagons in the street. Neither the tangible product nor the intellectual attainment is of any value – only the air and the light. There are idols in the galleries within upon whose sculptured features the hot eastern sun shone thousands of years since. They were made by human effort, however mistaken, and they were the outcome of human thought and handiwork. The doves fluttered about the temples in those days, full of air and light. They fluttered about the better temples of Greece and round the porticoes where philosophy was born. Still only the light, the sunlight, the air of heaven. We labour on and think, and carve our idols and the pen never ceases from its labour; but the lapse of centuries has left us in the same place. The doves who have not laboured nor travailed in thought possess the sunlight. Is not theirs the preferable portion?

Jefferies turned from the man-made gods that were housed in the British Museum to air and light, where he looked to find freedom. But what Jefferies was looking for could have come to him anywhere – in a crowded street, even a church. The freedom that nature-mystics look for beyond the human scene is like the spiritual realm of the religious, a human thought-construction. Seeking to escape yourself by chasing your own shadow is a vain pursuit. But if you look with eyes that are not covered with a film of thought, you may come on a scene that can only be seen once.

INFINITE CITIES

You need not look outside the human world to see a scene that humans have not made. The human world is itself unknowable to humans. The settlements they have made for themselves can be as impenetrable as the deepest forests.

I have known a man, dying a long way from London, sigh queerly for a sight of the gush of smoke that, on a platform of the Underground, one may see, escaping in great woolly clots up a circular opening, by a grimy, rusted iron shield, into the dim upper light. He wanted to see it again as others have wished to see once more the Bay of Naples, the olive groves of Catania. Another wanted – how very much he wanted! To see once more the carpet of pigeons on the gravel in front of a certain Museum steps; the odd top-hatted unpresentable figure of a battered man, holding a paper of bun crumbs, with pigeons on his shoulders, on his hands, crowding in between his feet and fluttering like an aureole of wings round his head.

London is a thing of these 'bits'. It is seldom that one sees at one time as much of it as one may always see of any country town . . . Viewed from a distance it is a cloud on the horizon. From the dark, further side of the Surrey hills at night, above the inky sky line of heather, of pine tops, of elm, one may see on the sky a brooding and sinister glow. That is London – manifesting itself on the clouds.

This passage comes from Ford Madox Ford's *The Soul of London* (1905), where the novelist, poet and literary critic applied to the city the method of

Impressionism that produced his most innovative work. In *The Good Soldier* (1915), Ford changed the nature of the novel by telling a story that had all the gaps and slippages of actual life and memory. The fiction of an omniscient spectator of the human scene was abandoned in favour of an attempt to recreate the elusiveness of experience. In the four-volume *Parade's End* (1924–8), possibly the greatest twentieth-century English novel, Ford applied a similar technique to recreating the impact of the Great War on life in England. In moving from narrative description to the irregularities of perception and memory, Ford was aiming for greater accuracy. Instead of fabricating a coherent narrative, he presents the experiences of a single individual; but the individual is a confluence of sensations rather than a continuing actor or observer.

Ford's literary Impressionism emerged around the same time as Impressionism in painting, and there are affinities between the two. As Impressionist painters tried not to represent things but rather to record sensations, Ford attempted to capture the transitory experiences that form our lives. Seeing the world as being made up of stable things is a kind of hallucination. Fast-vanishing scenes acquire the frozen fixity of illustrations in books and exhibits in museums. Literary Impressionism was an attempt at a new kind of realism.

Ford cites Tennyson as an example of the sort of writing he is criticizing:

> And bats went round in fragrant skies
> And wheeled or lit the filmy shapes
> That haunt the dusk, with ermine capes
> And woolly breasts and beady eyes.

Ford comments:

Now that is no doubt very good natural history, but it is certainly not Impressionism, since no one watching a bat at dusk could see the ermine, the wool or the beadiness of the eyes. These things you might read about in books, or observe in the museum or at the Zoological Gardens. Or you might pick up a dead bat on the road. But to import into the record of observations of one moment the observations of a moment altogether different is not Impressionism. For Impressionism is a thing altogether momentary ... any piece of Impressionism, whether it be prose, or verse, or painting, or sculpture, is the impression of a moment; it is not a sort of rounded, annotated record of a set of circumstances – it is the record of the recollection in your mind of a set of circumstances that happened ten years ago – or ten minutes. It might even be the impression of a moment – but it is the impression, not the corrected chronicle.

In this Impressionist view of things, the world that humans experience is not an imperfect representation of a reality that will some day be more fully known. Reflecting the nature of the animal that constructs it, the human world is a succession of fragments. No perfect perception of things is possible, since things change with each perception of them.

There are philosophers who will tell you that humanly constructed things can be known even if everything outside the human world is inaccessible. But the things humans make may also be unfathomable. A map can represent the physical structures of which a city is at any one time composed, but the city itself remains uncharted. This is not only because the city will have changed materially by the time the map appears. A map cannot contain the infinite places that the city contains, which come and go along with the people who pass through them. The chart is an abstraction, simplifying experiences that are incomparably more variegated. We think of cities as we think of ourselves, as stable things that recur throughout time, when in each case what is recurring is something insubstantial, a construction of thought that is fleeting and chimerical.

For Ford London was not an abiding place but a moving labyrinth:

Thought of from sufficiently afar, London offers to the mind singularly little of a picture. It is essentially 'town', and yet how little of a town, how much of an abstraction. One says, 'He knows his London', yet how little more will he know of London than what is actually 'his'. And, if by chance he were an astronomer, how much better he might know his solar system . . .

And, with its 'atmosphere' whatever it is, with its 'character' whatever it may be, with the odd touches that go to make up familiarity and the home-feeling, the shape of its policemen's helmets, the cachet of its shop fronts, the effects of light cast by steel lamps on the fog, on house fronts, on front garden trees, on park railings, all these little things going towards its atmosphere and character, that jumping-off place will remain for him, as it were, a glass through which he will afterwards view, a standard by which he will afterwards measure, the London that yet remains no one's.

Ford was not the first to suggest that London might be unknowable. Describing his opium-fuelled wanderings around the city, the early nineteenth-century essayist Thomas de Quincey confessed to having the impression that the streets through which he wandered were phantasms. Like his fellow opium-eater Samuel Coleridge much influenced by German Idealist philosophy, de Quincey held to a kind of transcendental occultism in which sensations were ciphers of spiritual things. But there is a gap that cannot be breached between Impressionism and the occult faith in a realm beyond what is revealed to the senses. The symbolic world that humans have made is not a hermetic text, which rightly interpreted gives a secret knowledge of things. Human symbols are a scattering of dust, spread over a world that is beyond understanding.

If Romantics turn from the things that humans have built in order to find something meaningful that humans have not made, Idealists return to the human world in order to escape the loss of meaning. Both are mistaken. Unknown to itself, the human mind creates worlds it cannot grasp. The places that are made by humans are as numinous and fugitive as those that appear in forest shade. Breaking the spell of diurnal perception, you can see landscapes in cities as unexpected as those that explorers discover in uncharted regions of the globe.

A CHURCHYARD COUGH AND A GREEN COAT

If you were consigned to an early grave, what would you do in the time that might be left? One such person chose to sit by a small pond:

Though it has the beautiful shape of a dew pond, it is not one. It is only a common pond supplied by the surface water of the wide downland gorges, and yet it has always seemed to me enchanted. I have often thought, as I have passed by it, that one day, under a special dispensation, I should receive from this little pool of water, from this small, green stoup of lustral water, a whisper as to the secret of life. It will be revealed to me, I have thought, as surely and as naturally as the presence of dew makes itself felt on folded twilight flowers found suddenly damp to the touch after the dry butterfly periods of a summer's day.

Always hoping for this hour of grace, I have loitered by the pond's edge at every season . . . It was on a soft evening of this last September that there came to me the breath of the knowledge that I sought . . . All was silent, all was expectant. The messenger for whom I had awaited was at last revealed.

It was a hare. I saw her from far away and did

not so much as venture to move a finger. She approached with uncertain steps, now advancing, now retreating, now frolicsome, now grave . . . Nearer and nearer she came. Was she actually intending to drink? Was it possible that I should see her lower her soft brown chin to the water ten yards from me? Surely if permitted to witness so delicate an operation, then at last I should receive the revelation I sought. The stillness of the evening was so profound that the fur of a field mouse's jacket brushing against the stems of its grassy jungle would have been audible, while against the sky, infinitely remote, the moon hung in utter calm . . .

I was suddenly awakened from my rapture. I had heard a sound, a sound sensitive and fresh as soft rain upon a leaf. It was the hare drinking.

Llewelyn Powys lived nearly all his adult life close to death. The younger brother of the better-known writers John Cowper Powys (1872–1963) and Theodore Powys (1875–1953) and one of eleven children of the Reverend Charles Francis Powys, Llewelyn learnt in 1909, at the age of twenty-five, that he was suffering from pulmonary tuberculosis.

The shock of discovering myself to be really ill had the strangest effect on me . . . I acted as if death were not the end of every child born into the world, but an event which in some mysterious way had been reserved for me alone . . . I liked to get what sensation I could out of it; and yet, at the same time, deep in my heart, I refused to realise how grave my sickness was. I liked to talk about dying, but I had no mind to die . . . In every possible way I dramatised my situation. My head became completely turned, and I chattered at Death like a little grey squirrel who is up a tree out of harm's way.

Llewelyn's brother John came from Paris to see him in Dorset, entering his room before daylight. They would talk until morning, Llewelyn in a whisper so as not to harm his lungs. Theodore, who travelled from his village near by, seemed preoccupied with the prospect that he might catch Llewelyn's complaint: 'He sat by the open window, inhaling the fresh air, as he uttered a thousand whimsical and fantastical observations.' Another visitor was an old stonemason. 'He sat by my bedside, his whole demeanour displaying that particular exultation one human being feels at seeing another caught in an evil trap. "*You have a churchyard cough*," he said . . . These words, I say, fairly made me jump, bringing home to me, as they did . . . that it was I, and I alone, who, when all my dramatisations and sensationalisms were over, would be spending cold nights, cold years, cold centuries, alone in a cold elm-wood coffin.'

Seeking treatment for his illness, Powys left England in December 1909 for Clavadel in Switzerland, where he spent two years in a sanatorium. While convalescing he had recurrent dreams of dying.

I had done this since my childhood, but during this period these insubstantial images would be more palpable, more real, than ever before. I would be wandering over some obscure dream-landscape, when I would be suddenly aware of a certain smell assailing my nostrils. It would be sweet and at the same time foul. 'Ha!' I would say to myself, 'the smell of mortality, the smell of decaying human flesh!' And immediately the ground upon which I was standing would sink under me and I would find myself struggling in a graveyard which was giving way in all directions . . . And I discovered, in after-years when I have approached with too much confidence the corpses of those I have loved, that the smell of my dream *was* the smell of dead human bodies, a smell subtly different from that which rises from dead cattle.

With death all around him, Powys felt released from the sexual repression that ran through English middle-class life at the time. As a result his time in the Swiss sanatorium, where these middle-class mores were unknown, was not as unhappy as might be

supposed. 'I was overjoyed to find myself in so fortunate a playground, and felt, in truth, the infinite
content we might imagine experienced by a butterfly,
a red admiral, let us say, which after a weary flight
across the asphalt streets of a city, finds itself in the
happy seclusion of a garden full of geraniums . . .' He
differed from some of his companions in that he still
wanted passionately to live. Yet he risked his health
again and again in playful encounters with fellow
sufferers who might still have been infectious.

For the rest of his life Llewelyn was an ardent pro-
ponent of sexual freedom and a determined opponent
of Christianity, which he opposed partly for its com-
plicity in sexual repression. He saw himself as a
disciple of Lucretius, though without accepting the
Roman poet's Epicurean belief that sex should be
avoided as a threat to mental tranquillity. Many of
his later writings are an impassioned defence of materialism. 'The possible annihilation of matter,' he
wrote, 'the possible annihilation of the universe –
here indeed is a hypothesis upon which to found the
philosophy of our lives.' He was adamant that rejecting religion meant renouncing any idea of order in
the world.

It is not only belief in God that must be abandoned, not only all hope of life after death, but all
trust in an ordained moral order. It is as plain as

THE SILENCE OF ANIMALS

the sun that existence as we know it can be under the supervision of no scrupulous deity . . . The absence of moral order unconnected with human manners is certain. We must be prepared to take our bearings without a compass and with the slippery deck of our life-vessel sliding away under our feet. Dogmatic nihilists, profoundly sceptical of all good, we are put to our resources like shipwrecked seamen. We have no sense of direction, and recognise without dispute that beyond the margin of our own scant moment all is lost.

From the stray sayings of Jesus – 'an original and passionate poet' – St Paul contrived a life-denying religion. Rather than fighting it, Powys advised leaving behind the faith that Paul invented: 'Let it go. What does it matter? It is all the same. Let the midges sing, let the bees murmur with blunt insect snouts set deep in honey. The birds asleep in the branches of trees, the midnight insects performing obscure missions among the stems of single grasses, were then as they are today utterly removed from the fantasies that stirred this man's mind.' Humans are 'dream cattle, images of breath, passing shadows that move swiftly across the world's pastures to a graveyard where, at a single clap, eternity is as a day and a day as eternity'.

Though he was an enemy of traditional religion,

Powys was not blind to its beauty. 'Sometimes, of an early Sunday morning, I would enter the old grey church to take the sacrament . . . And as I knelt with bowed head to partake of the beautiful, antique ritual, I would try to conceive what inner secret the wild rumour held, so that it could survive generation after generation, wherever two or three might be gathered together. And with the curious peace of the place all about me, with the cold, bare trees in the churchyard hedge visible through the leaded window-panes . . . I would feel half-inclined to believe also. Why not?' Though he never ceased to be amazed at the spread of Christianity, or to regret that it had succeeded in converting so many, he did not attribute this success to human stupidity. Religion was a poetic response to unchanging human realities – above all, the fact of death.

Returning to Dorset when his sickness seemed to have retreated, he met an old wood-cutter walking in a country lane.

'Well, I'll be damned!' he exclaimed. 'I never looked to see ye back, Master Llewelyn, 'cept as a corpse, if you follow my meaning' . . . The old wood-cutter looked me up and down, from the hat on my head to the boots on my feet, stained yellow with buttercup-dust. 'Ye may linger out the summer,' he said judiciously; 'but you'll never get rid of that cough. The doctors say they can cure ye, but they cannot do it. They can patch ye up, maybe, but never fear, you'll soon be a-wearing a green coat.' By 'wearing a green coat', he referred, I knew, to the green grass, which he was convinced would soon be growing over my grave.

The wood-cutter was right that Powys would not be cured but mistaken in thinking he would soon be dead. In 1914 Powys sailed for British East Africa, where one of his brothers was farming, and spent five years working as a stock farmer himself. Later, he would make a name for himself in America by publishing a series of articles describing his time in Africa. His life there only toughened his philosophy: 'Africa, like one of her own black-maned lions, laps up the life-blood of all the delicate illusions that have for so long danced before the eyes of men and made them happy. Truth alone is left alive. What was suspected in Europe is made plain here: *at the bottom of the well of Life there is no hope.* Under Scorpio, under the Southern Cross, and in the clear light of this passionless, tropical sunshine, the hollow emptiness of the world's soul is made plain: *the surface is everything, below there is nothing.*' Rather than perturbing him, the discovery that there was nothing beneath the surface of things made him all the more determined to enjoy life.

After returning to Dorset again he set off with his brother John in 1919 to try to make a living in America as a writer and lecturer. Temperamentally unsuited to lecturing (unlike his brother), he made so little money from writing that at one point he considered living in one of the rooms advertised at twenty-five cents a night at a hotel on Sixth Avenue in New York – desolate little cubicles, opening catacomb-like on to a central passage. 'With a feeling of infinite nostalgia I remembered how once I had ridden over wide African plains, where the hoofs of my stallion had clicked against the bones of lions; where there had been places as removed from mankind and the traps they lay for one another, that a sow rhinoceros could suckle her young, completely ignorant that there existed in the world an erect anthropoid as unprecedented in its cunning and ferocity as *homo sapiens*.'

In 1925 Powys returned to England and settled on a remote spot on the Dorset coast accompanied by Alyse Gregory, formerly editor of the American literary journal the *Dial*, whom he had married in New York in 1924. The two travelled together widely – back to America where he had at last acquired a reputation through his recollection of his time in Africa, *Ebony and Ivory* and *Black Laughter*, to Palestine and Capri, to America again and the West Indies, back to Dorset and then again to Switzerland.

Born in 1884, he died of a haemorrhaged ulcer in December 1939.

Powys's death seems to have been much as he visualized it in *Love and Death: An Imaginary Autobiography*, published in May 1939:

> Presently I realized that Alyse must have sent the nurse away, for we were alone together. My fever had left me. I felt cold, and shuddered. My mind, however, remained clear. I was dying and I knew it. Deprived of the residue of my day I must relinquish now my private breath. It had come to me at last, this dread moment. It had come but I felt no fear . . . Death, I thought, is not as terrible as I expected . . . My chest was heaving. A deeper blackness than ever rolled in over me, submerging my being, whelming it in a flood of utter darkness, a darkness innocent of sensation, innocent of thought; a darkness careless of all save a blind, unenvious commerce with the dust of unending ages.

In Switzerland, a few hours before he died, Powys said to his wife: 'I wish I were the sweet web of dust.' A year later, back in Dorset, Alyse wrote: 'Our origin is an animal one and we return to the dust – the fantasies of our brain are but thistledown in the wind. I like formality, finesse, subtlety of behaviour and thought, and at the same time I know that life is *nothing* at all – a fanfare, a rook's wing, gone like a boy's whistle.' She lived on for over a quarter of a century, much of the time happy, being visited by friends from all over the world and enjoying the wild scenery around the house where she and her husband had lived together. Becoming too frail for the walks that living there involved, she left and went to live inland in 1957. Ten years later she killed herself, swallowing a fatal powder after lying down on a cloak her husband used to wear.

Powys did not take his own life, but he did not struggle when it was taken from him. He refused an operation recommended for him by his doctors. 'They are dragging me the wrong way. I have had a happy life and I want to die in the end like a follower of Epicurus.' A week before he died, he had written to a friend: 'I have had a happy life for half a century in sunshine.'

What was it that Powys pursued throughout his life, as he fled the prospect of an early death? Certainly it was not immortality. He shared the feeling of the Imagist poet F. S. Flint that human beings are not fit to be immortal:

> Immortal? . . . No,
> They cannot be, these people,
> nor I.

Tired faces,
eyes that have never seen the world,
bodies that have never lived in air,
lips that have never minted speech,
they are the clipped and garbled,
blocking the high-way . . .
Immortal? . . .
In a wood,
Watching the shadow of a bird,
Leap from frond to frond of bracken,
I am immortal.
But these?

Being mortal was not a punishment for Powys, though he hated the thought of dying. The fact that he was never far from death left him free to follow his fancy, which was the sensation of life itself.

A VANISHING ACT

Describing M. Monde, a respectable businessman who on his forty-eighth birthday suddenly disappears, leaving behind him his business and his family – a son and daughter and the woman he had married after leaving his first wife – Georges Simenon wrote of a man who 'had laid all ghosts, who had lost all shadows, and who stared you in the eyes with cold serenity'. He does so of his own free will, and yet it seems to him that he had no choice. 'There was no inner conflict, no decision to be reached, indeed nothing was ever decided at all.' When he takes a large sum of money from the safe and steps out into the street, he has no clear plan of action. After changing into workman's clothes and having his moustache shaved off he checks into a cheap hotel, then in the morning takes the train to Marseilles.

When he wakes up in another cheap room, near the city's harbour, he realizes that he has been weeping. 'They were no ordinary tears. They gushed in a warm, endless flow from some deep spring, they gathered behind the barrier of his lashes and then poured freely down his cheeks, not in separate drops but in zigzagging rivulets like those that run down windowpanes on rainy days, and the patch of wetness beside his chin spread ever wider on his pillow.' His tears are not because of the bare room but because of the life he has had:

He was lucid, not with an everyday lucidity, the sort one admits, but on the contrary the sort of which one subsequently feels ashamed, perhaps because it confers on supposedly commonplace things the grandeur ascribed to them by poetry and religion. What was streaming from his whole being, through his two eyes, was all the fatigue accumulated during forty-eight years, and if they were gentle tears, it was because the ordeal was over.

He had given up. He had stopped struggling. He had hurried from far away – the train journey no longer existed, there was only a sense of endless flight – he had hurried here, towards the sea which, vast and blue, more intensely alive than any human being, the soul of the world, was breathing peacefully close to him.

Woken from his dream by the sound of a quarrel in the next room, he falls in with a girl – Julie – who gets a job as a hostess in a casino. In a few days he is living with her and working in a nightclub, where he is paid to watch the staff through a peep-hole to check if they are cheating. A few days later the parcel containing the money he had taken from the safe, which he put on top of the wardrobe in his room, is gone. Now he has nothing, and having changed his name to Désiré Chouet – a name he had seen over a cobbler's shop – he lives as others do.

M. Monde has not found the freedom he was looking for. The world he finds on the margins of society is not so different from the one he has rejected, only more hard-pressed. Still, life is different for Désiré. The light has changed: 'The light was the same as that which pervades sheltered creeks of the Mediterranean:

it was sunlight, he realised, but sunlight diluted, dif-
fused, sometimes decomposed as though in a prism,
suddenly violet for instance or green, the intense green
of the legendary, elusive green ray.'

He is not disappointed or depressed. He knows
who stole his money – a maid who had looked at him
with hostility since the theft, whom he greets with
exaggerated courtesy whenever they meet.

Monsieur Monde felt no anger, no resentment, no
regret. About his fourteenth or fifteenth year, while
he was at the Lycée, he had gone through a period
of acute mysticism following a Lenten fast. He had
devoted his days and part of his nights to spiritual
perfection, and he had happened to keep a photo-
graph of himself at that date . . . He looked thinner
and rather scornful, with a smile whose sweetness
infuriated him later, when the reaction set in . . .
And though his once rosy complexion was now
sallow, he would look with some complacency,
when the occasion arose, at the reflection of a face
that spoke not only of serenity but of a secret joy,
an almost morbid delectation.

Working at the spy-hole he sees his ex-wife, now a
morphine addict, in the nightclub. They meet and
they travel back to Paris, where he arranges for her to
be treated. At the same time he returns to his family

without offering any explanation for his absence. He is not the same person as before. While persuading his first wife to come with him and be placed under the care of a doctor, something had happened to him:

He was certainly not a disembodied spirit. He was still Monsieur Monde, or Désiré, more likely Désiré . . . No! it didn't matter . . . He was a man who, for a long time, had endured man's estate without being conscious of it, as others endure an illness of which they are unaware. He had always been a man among other men and like them he had struggled, jostling amid the crowd, now feebly and now resolutely, without knowing whither he was going.

And now, in the moonlight he suddenly saw life differently, as though with the aid of some miraculous X-ray.

Everything that had counted previously, the whole integument and flesh and the outward appearance of it all had ceased to exist, and what there was in its place . . .

But there! It wasn't worth talking about it to Julie or to anyone else. The thing was *incommunicable*.

What had he come to know that he had not known before? Lying in bed in the hotel in Marseilles, diving in and out of sleep, he felt he had discovered something. But what was it that he had discovered?

He turned over heavily on his hard bed that smelt of sweat. He had grown used to the smell of his own sweat again, just as when he had been a child. For too many years, for the greater part of his life, he had forgotten the smell of sweat, the smell of the sun, all those living smells of which people who go about their business are no longer conscious, and he wondered if that were not the reason why . . .

He was close to a truth, a discovery, he had begun to dive down again, then something brought him back to the surface . . .

What M. Monde has discovered cannot be put into words. A negative epiphany in which the meanings of everyday life fall away, it comes and goes in a flash. But what M. Monde sees is not without value, for it leaves him a different man.

M. Monde Vanishes is one of the *romans durs* – what Simenon called 'hard novels' to distinguish them from the hundreds of popular thrillers he also wrote – in which the creator of Inspector Maigret explored the moods of unsettlement that undermine the most seemingly solid lives.

The subject matter of these hard tales is the human soul, but there is very little psychology in Simenon's account of his characters. M. Monde exists in the impressions that move him to act. When he abandons his bourgeois comforts for the seeming romance of the *demi-monde*, the reader is not told what motives possessed the businessman. Instead we learn that M. Monde did not know himself why he was leaving. Though we learn something of the thoughts that trouble him when he sleeps, we are told little of M. Monde's state of mind. We discover that when he was in his early teens he had a period of piety. Whether that piety has anything to do with his sudden renunciation of the settled life is left open.

It is as if M. Monde is composed from the settings in which he finds himself. Though he hardly knew what he did, the move he made was his own doing – an act of impulse. The stranger he becomes emerges as if from nothing – a response to the sights, sounds and smells he encounters when he sheds his old life. Simenon's tales carry no moral lesson. But if there is an idea at work in them, it is that the impressions through which we pass are more real than the selves we think are authors of our lives.

As in all of Simenon's writings, religion is not rejected but ignored. M. Monde looks back on his teenage austerities with tender scorn, and there is nothing to suggest that he yearns for any kind of redemption. What he is seeking is a kind of freedom – the kind that comes when you are no longer ruled by the laws of memory.

In his study of Proust, Samuel Beckett wrote:

The laws of memory are subject to the more general laws of habit. Habit is a compromise effected between the individual and his environment, or between the individual and his own organic eccentricities, the guarantor of a dull inviolability, the lightning-conductor of his existence. Habit is the ballast that chains the dog to his vomit. Breathing is habit. Life is habit. Or rather life is a succession of habits, since the individual is a succession of individuals . . . The creation of the world did not take place once and for all, but takes place every day. Habit then is the generic term for the countless treaties concluded between the countless subjects that constitute the individual and their countless correlative objects. The periods of transition that separate consecutive adaptations (because by no expedient of macabre transubstantiation can the grave sheets serve as swaddling clothes) represent the perilous zones in the life of the individual, dangerous, precarious, painful, mysterious and fertile, when for a moment the boredom of living is replaced by the suffering of being.

The world in which you live from day to day is made from habit and memory. The perilous zones are the times when the self, also made from habit and memory, gives way. Then, if only for a moment, you may become something other than you have been.

THE STRANGER IN THE WINGS

The patron saint of humanism is an enigmatic figure. We cannot know what Socrates was really like, since the image we have of him was fashioned by Plato. The founder of western philosophy may have been a sophist, who rather than accepting that he knew nothing believed there was nothing worth knowing; or a late practitioner of shamanism, whose glimpses of truth came from an inner oracle. He may even have been as Plato describes him, a rationalist mystic who believed that human beings – an initiated few, at any rate – could gain access to a realm beyond time.

It does not much matter who or what Socrates may have been, since the power he has over the mind is the power of myth. The Socratic inheritance is a number of articles of faith, which in one form or another have shaped humanist thinking. The idea that human evil is a type of error, which will fade away as knowledge advances; that the good life must be an examined life; that the practice of reason can enable human beings to shape their own fates – these questionable claims have been repeated as unchallengeable axioms ever since Socrates acquired the status of a humanist saint. Nietzsche, who attacked Socrates fiercely without ever ceasing to admire and revere him, wrote: 'One is obliged to see in Socrates the single point around which so-called world history turns and twists.'

If only because of the implicit assumption that it is European thought that shapes world history, it is an extravagant claim. Yet it is true that much in modern thinking rests on Socratic premises. When he attacked Socrates as the ultimate source of humanism, Nietzsche looked back to an archaic pre-philosophical Greek culture that may never have existed in the Dionysian form he imagined. But when he writes, 'the image of the dying Socrates, the man elevated over the fear of death through knowledge and reasoning, is the heraldic shield hung above the entrance gate of science in order to remind everybody of its purpose, namely to make existence appear intelligible and so justified,' Nietzsche accurately describes the faith by which those in the west who think they have given up religion actually live.

As Nietzsche understood, it is a tenet of this faith that tragedy is not a final fact: what we call tragic is only a type of error, whose incidence and effects can be reduced over time. With reasonable forethought, tragedy can be avoided, or else – if it proves to be inescapable – used to stir human aspirations in future. No doubt human beings will always suffer loss and sadness. But human life need not be tragic. For if tragedy can always be prevented or redeemed, there is in the end no tragedy.

THE SILENCE OF ANIMALS

This view was given to the mythological Greek Theban king Pentheus by the American poet Robinson Jeffers (1887–1962) in 'The Humanist's Tragedy', a short verse rendition of Euripides' play *The Bacchae*. For a time influential, then intensely controversial and finally almost forgotten, Jeffers remains one of the twentieth century's most interesting critics of humanism. He reworked the Greek drama as a poetic image, intimating that tragedy goes with being human and yet there is something beyond tragedy.

A believer in reason, Pentheus banned the worship of Dionysus, the god of wine, ecstasy and excess. Having lured Pentheus' mother along with the other Theban women to a mountain where they engage in Bacchic rites, Dionysus then lures Pentheus to the mountain, where the king is torn apart by the revellers. Possessed by the god, Pentheus' mother is among those who kill the king. Believing it to be the head of a lion, she brings her son's head to the royal court. The trance wears off, and she realizes what she has done. Ruined, she and her sisters go into exile. Only a blind old man remains.

Jeffers describes how Pentheus – 'Not like a beast borne on the flood of passion, boat without oars, but mindful of all his dignity as a human being, a king and a Greek' – is tricked into witnessing the Bacchic orgy:

Without awe, without pleasure,
As a man spies on noxious beasts, he standing
hidden spied on
The rabid choir of the God.
They had pine-cone-tipped wands, they went half-
naked, they were hoarse with insane song; foam from
their mouths,
mingled
With wine and sweat, ran down their bodies. O fools,
boats
Without oars borne on the flood of passion,
Forgetting utterly all the dignity of man, the pride of
the only
self-commanding animal,
That captains his own soul and controls even
Fate, for a space. The only animal that turns means
to an end.

Rather than strengthening Pentheus' faith in reason, the sight of the frenzy throws the king into
confusion:

'What end? Oh, but what end?'
It cried under his mind, 'Increase the city? Subdue the
earth?
Breed slaves and cattle, and one's own
Off-shots, fed and secure? Ah fruitful-fruitless
Generations forever and ever . . . For pleasure' – he
spat on

The earth – 'the slight collectible pleasure
Surplus to pain? . . .'
              'The generations', he thought suddenly,
'aspire. They better; they climb . . . Had I
forgotten the end
of being? To increase the power, the collectedness
and dignity of
          man. – A more collected and dignified
Creature,' he groaned, 'to die and stink.'

Pentheus wants to remain in human collectedness.
But the god appears – 'like a tall ship / breasting
through water' – and says softly to the worshippers:

              'When you are dead you
        become part of peace; let no man
Dream more of death; there is neither sight nor hear-
ing nor any
          wonder; none of us gods enters it.
    You become part of peace, but *having*
no part: as if a flute-player
Should make beauty but hear none, being deaf and
senseless.
          But living if you will
It is possible for you to break prison of yourselves
and enter the
Nature of things and use the beauty.

Wine and lawlessness, art and music, love, self-
torture, religion,
Are means but not needful, contemplation will do it.
Only
To break human collectedness.'

The god articulates Jeffers's view of things, which
he called Inhumanism:

> a shifting of emphasis and significance from man
> to not-man; the rejection of human solipsism and
> recognition of the transhuman magnificence . . .
> This manner of thought and feeling is neither mis-
> anthropic nor pessimist, though two or three peo-
> ple have said so and may again. It involves no
> falsehoods, and is a means of maintaining sanity in
> tricky times; it has objective truth and value. It
> offers a reasonable detachment as a rule of con-
> duct, instead of love, hate and envy. It neutralizes
> fanaticism and wild hopes; but it provides mag-
> nificence for the religious instinct, and satisfies our
> need to admire greatness and rejoice in beauty.

The attitude that Jeffers promoted, and tried and
failed himself to practise, involved 'the devaluation of
human illusions, the turning outward from man to
what is boundlessly greater'. Humans needed this

turn outwards if they were not to be forever turning on each other: 'if in some future civilization the dreams of Utopia should incredibly be realized, and men were actually freed from want and fear, then all the more they would need this sanctuary, against the deadly emptiness and insignificance of their lives, at leisure fully appreciated. Man, much more than baboon or wolf, is an animal formed for conflict; his life seems meaningless to him without it. Only a clear shift of meaning and emphasis from man to what is not man, nor a man-dreamed God, a projection of man, can enable him in the long run to endure peace.'

Retreating in 1914 to the wild coast of northern California, Jeffers built a house of stone near Carmel for himself and his wife (who died in 1950) and lived there the rest of his life. In semi-seclusion Jeffers struggled to remain aloof from the human conflicts whose insignificance he preached. He wanted to revive the sense of tragedy; but he proved unable to see tragedy when it was being enacted in front of him. Rightly judging the First World War a catastrophe, he could not see that the Second World War followed as a tragic necessity. Supporting American isolation, he struggled to adopt a pose of detachment:

> even the P-38s and the Flying
> Fortresses are as natural as horse-flies;

It is only that man, his griefs and rages, are not
  what they
seem to man, not great and shattering, but really

Too small to produce any disturbance. This is good.
This is the sanity, the mercy. It is true that the
Murdered
Cities leave marks in the earth for a certain time,
  like
Fossil rain-prints in shale, equally beautiful.

Jeffers's attempt to find beauty in the desperate
conflict that followed the attack on Pearl Harbor
destroyed his reputation as a poet. Appearing in
1948, the poems seemed to confirm the accusations
of his critics, who regarded him as an enemy of civilization. In demanding American isolation in a war
against a hideous version of modern barbarism, the
reclusive poet was badly mistaken. Yet in thinking
that when it is entirely immersed in itself the human
animal goes mad, Jeffers was right.

He was criticized in a more balanced way by the
Polish poet Czesław Miłosz, who lived for a time not
far from Carmel, and while admiring his courage
rejected Jeffers's – and any – attempt to look out of
the human world. Miłosz noted that Jeffers 'was a
religious writer, though not in the sense that his
father, a Calvinist pastor, would have approved'.

It is a shrewd observation, but Jeffers did not altogether abandon his father's faith. Like Nietzsche – whose father was also a pastor – Jeffers never left Christianity behind. Instead of thinking of the universe as emanating from God, he saw the universe as a purposeless process – but one that still had to be worshipped. Just as the ordinary pleasures of life had to be renounced for the sake of his father's punitive deity, for Jeffers human feelings had to be sacrificed for the sake of a pantheist divinity. Jeffers loved the ocean, and lived near it, because the sea represented the freedom from human concerns of which he dreamt. Miłosz preferred the customs of the Catholic village of his childhood, where people carved suns and moons on the joints of crosses, to Jeffers's cosmic psalm. As Miłosz wrote in a poem he dedicated to Jeffers,

> The earth teaches
> more than does the nakedness of
> elements. No one with impunity
> gives himself the eyes of a god.

In trying to give himself the eyes of a god Jeffers was not departing only from Christianity. He was also at odds with the pagans he wanted to emulate. Pagan thinkers such as Seneca and Lucretius aspired to the passionless calm of the cosmos. They did not imagine they could become the cosmos while still living. They accepted mortality as a gift. Jeffers wanted to celebrate tragedy, and like Nietzsche preached *amor fati*: fate should be embraced with joy. But the pagans did not see fate as something that must be loved or worshipped. Marcus Aurelius counselled resignation to fate – not *amor fati*. Seneca advised forcing fate to fight on equal terms and, if it looks like having the upper hand, denying fate its victory by taking your own life.

The Dionysian self-immolation that Nietzsche read back into the archaic Greeks and that Jeffers wanted to revive was actually a Christian embrace of sacrifice and submission. For that very reason, neither Nietzsche nor Jeffers was able to recover the sense of tragedy. For all the agony that it expresses, the cross is not a tragic symbol. Tragedy there would have been if Jesus were to die defeated and for ever. Instead he returns from the dead and the world is redeemed. With their hope of progress, modern anti-Christians remain disciples of an anti-tragic faith.

But it is not only Christianity that denies tragedy. So does the other main current of the western tradition that comes from Socrates and Plato. Like some of the traditions of eastern mysticism, Platonism dissolves the self into an imagined oneness.

In 'Credo', a poem that may have emerged from his meetings in the mid-1930s with the Indian teacher

Jiddu Krishnamurti, Jeffers pointed to the differences between his own and eastern mysticism:

> My friend from Asia has powers and magic, he
>   picks a blue leaf from the young blue-
>   gum
> And gazing upon it, gathering and quieting
> The God in his mind, creates an ocean more
>   real than the ocean, the salt, the
>   actual
> Appalling presence, the power of the waters.
> He believes that nothing is real except as we
>   make it. I humbler have found in my
>   blood
> Bred west of Caucasus a harder mysticism . . .
>   . . . The mind
> Passes, the eye closes, the spirit is a passage;
> The beauty of things was born before eyes and
>   sufficient to itself; the heartbreaking
>   beauty
> Will remain when there is no heart to break
>   for it.

Jeffers meant his 'harder mysticism' to be an alternative to the introspective quest of mystics who, looking within themselves for traces of God, still think of humans as being at the centre of things. Looking outwards from humanity, Jeffers was taking a necessary turn; but when he writes of undying beauty he shows that his mysticism is a traditional, other-worldly kind. Jeffers wanted to avoid identifying human ideas with timeless reality as Plato had done; but, like the Greek philosopher, he projected a human response to the world into the nature of things. The beauty he says will survive any human eye is the harmony that Plato envisioned subsisting out of time – the same harmony that Socrates imagined could cancel human misfortune. For the founder of western philosophy, *Logos* – the universal reason that spoke through him – secured those who followed it from any ultimate loss.

Unlike his modern disciples Socrates had no thought of progress: salvation was not an historical event but absorption into a timeless realm. One reason Socrates never challenged the justice of the sentence that condemned him to death was that he thought the most essential part of him could not die. This Greek conception of a perfect spiritual reality was assimilated into theism, where it became part of the idea of God. Jeffers's was not the godless mysticism to which he aspired, but a transfiguration of Christian and Platonic religion.

Without realizing it Jeffers was renewing the Socratic faith that, together with Christianity, has shaped western humanism. Mixing a Greek idea of reason as giving access to timeless truths with a Christian view of salvation in history has not produced anything like a coherent synthesis; but the resulting humanism – secular and religious – has formed the central western tradition. Alongside this, there have always been voices hinting that life can be lived well without metaphysical comfort: ancient European dramatists and sceptics, early modern intellectual adventurers like Montaigne and in more recent times Mauthner and Freud, thinkers who were not afraid to doubt the worth of thought.

If the human mind can ever be released from myth it is not through science, still less through philosophy, but in moments of contemplation. When Wallace Stevens describes a Russian émigré looking at a dish of peaches, the Russian touches the peaches with more than his mind:

> With my whole body I taste these peaches,
> I touch them and smell them. Who speaks? . . .
> Who speaks? But it must be that I,
> That animal, that Russian, that exile . . .
>
> . . . I did not know
> That such ferocities could tear
> One self from another, as these peaches do.

The revelation that comes from looking at the peaches changes 'that I, that animal', a poor beast that is richer than it knows. The self that appears in the Russian when he is looking at the peaches is unknown to him. Seeing the peaches with a stranger's eyes, he is engaged in contemplation of a kind other than that of which religious mystics speak. He breaks out from the prison of his ordinary self not into a great oneness but into an outward world he has not seen before. The vision may bring peace, or fierce sadness. Either way it is an interval in the life of the mind.

Contemplation can be understood as an activity that aims not to change the world or to understand it, but simply to let it be. Being receptive in this way is no easy matter. John Baker's decade-long pursuit of the hawk and Llewelyn Powys's lifelong struggle to regain a vision at a pond involved a resolute refusal of distractions and obstacles. But the epiphanies that resulted were not a product of the intense concentration that necessarily preceded them. The wilful opening of the mind to the senses is a prelude to events that cannot be made to happen.

Like that of religious mystics, contemplation of this kind involves nullifying the self. But not with the aim of entering any higher self – a figment left behind by an animal mind. God-seeking mystics want this figment to guide them in a new way of living. They are right in thinking that a life made up only of action is the pursuit of phantoms; but so is life passed on a fictive frontier between two worlds. The needy animal that invented the other world does not go away, and the result of trying to leave the creature behind is to live instead with its ghost.

Godless contemplation is a more radical and transient condition: a temporary respite from the all-too-human world, with nothing particular in mind. In most traditions the life of contemplation promises redemption from being human: in Christianity, the end of tragedy and a glimpse of the divine comedy; in Jeffers's pantheism, the obliteration of the self in an ecstatic unity. Godless mysticism cannot escape the finality of tragedy, or make beauty eternal. It does not dissolve inner conflict into the false quietude of any oceanic calm. All it offers is mere being. There is no redemption from being human. But no redemption is needed. As Louis MacNeice wrote:

> If there has been no spiritual change of kind
> Within our species since Cro-Magnon Man
> And none is looked for while the millennia
>   cool,
> Yet each of us has known mutations in the
>   mind
> When the world jumped and what had been a
>   plan

Dissolved and rivers gushed from what seemed
      a pool
For every static world that you or I impose
Upon the real one must crack at times and new
Patterns from new disorders open like a rose
And old assumptions yield to new sensations.
The Stranger in the wings is waiting for his
      cue . . .

Acknowledgements

This book could not have been written without the help and support of many people. Simon Winder, my editor at Penguin, gave me encouragement at every stage of my work on it, and his comments on the text have been invaluable. Tracy Bohan, my agent at the Wylie Agency, gave me all the support a writer could ask for, together with advice from which I have benefited greatly. Adam Phillips's comments on the text made a vital contribution to the shape of the book. Bryan Appleyard introduced me to Wallace Stevens, whose poetry has stirred me in many ways, with results that appear in the book. Conversations with John Banville, Richard Holloway, Gerard Lemos, Paul Schutze, Will Self, Geoffrey Smith and Jon Stokes entered into the thoughts that are voiced here. As ever, my deepest debt is to my wife Mieko.

Responsibility for the contents of the book, including any errors it contains, remains mine alone.

John Gray

Notes

EPIGRAPH

'The seasons are': John Ashbery, 'Syringa', *Selected Poems*, Manchester, Carcanet, 2002, 245.

CHAPTER 1: AN OLD CHAOS

1 'The highly civilized': Arthur Koestler, *Darkness at Noon*, London, Vintage, 2005, 183–4.

2 'Kayerts was hanging': Joseph Conrad, 'An Outpost of Progress', *Almayer's Folly and Tales of Unrest*, London, Dent, 1972, 117, 94–5, 114, 116, 91, 92, 94, 100, 89, 91, 116.

4 'Before the Congo': G. Jean-Aubry, *Joseph Conrad: Life and Letters*, 2 vols, Garden City, NY, Doubleday, 1927, 1:141.

4 'They lived like': Conrad, 'An Outpost of Progress', 87, 95, 116.

9 'She hears, upon': Wallace Stevens, 'Sunday Morning', *The Palm at the End of the Mind: Selected Poems and a*

Play by Wallace Stevens, ed. Holly Stevens, New York, Vintage Books, 1960, 8.

10 'He was in a long': Joseph Conrad, *The Secret Agent*, Oxford and New York, Oxford University Press, 1983, 81–2, 311.

11 'It is astonishing': Norman Lewis, *Naples '44: An Intelligence Officer in the Italian Labyrinth*, London, Eland, 2002, 43, 12, 51–2, 126, 168, 49.

13 'Lewis's life was': See Julian Evans, *Semi-Invisible Man: The Life of Norman Lewis*, London, Jonathan Cape, 2008.

16 'I spent many': Norman Lewis, *I Came, I Saw*, London, Picador, 1994, 321–3.

19 Life in Naples: For Malaparte's life, see Dan Hofstadter's Afterword to Malaparte's *Kaputt*, trans. Cesare Foligno, New York, New York Review Books, 2005, 431–7.

20 'Before the liberation': Curzio Malaparte, *The Skin*, trans. David Moore, New York, Avon Books, 1965, 51–3, 48.

22 'I had never felt': Malaparte, *Kaputt*, 416.

24 'The lake looked': Ibid., 55.

24 'Much of the time': Malaparte's dispatches from the Eastern Front can be read in English in Curzio Malaparte, *The Volga Rises in Europe*, Edinburgh, Birlinn, 2000, 173, 267, 239–40.

26 'In my youth': Arthur Koestler, *The Invisible Writing: Autobiography 1931–53*, London, Collins/Hamish Hamilton, 1954, 15, 353, 351–2.

28 'Something had clicked': Arthur Koestler, *Arrow in the Blue: Autobiography*, London, Collins/Hamish Hamilton, 1952, 236–7.

31 'Perhaps Hitler's genius': Arthur Koestler, *Scum of the Earth*, London, Eland, 2006, 212, 155. It is now known that Maeterlinck's book was plagiarized from the Afrikaans writer Eugene Marais's *The Soul of the White Ant* (1925).

34 'Everything in our': Stefan Zweig, *The World of Yesterday*, Lincoln, Nebr. and London, University of Nebraska Press, 1964, 1–2.

35 'The railway station': Joseph Roth, *The Emperor's Tomb*, trans. John Hoare, London, Granta Books, 1999, 35–6.

38 'the so-called "nationality question"': Joseph Roth, 'The Bust of the Emperor', *Collected Shorter Fiction*, trans. Michael Hoffman, London, Granta Books, 2001, 241–2.

41 'You are a slow': George Orwell, *1984*, London, Penguin Books, 1987, 263, 266, 267.

42 'Nazi theory specifically': George Orwell, 'Looking Back on the Spanish War', *Essays*, London, Penguin Books, 2000, 224–5.

43 'Industrialization went forward': Eugene Lyons, *Assignment in Utopia*, New York, Harcourt Brace, 1937, 240.

45 Jones was expelled: An account of Jones's life and death is presented by Margaret Siriol Colley in *Gareth Jones: A Manchukuo Incident*, Nottingham, Alphagraphics, 2001. A radio documentary on Jones, *But They are Only Russians*, was broadcast by BBC Radio 4 on 13 January 2012.

46 'At provincial railroad': Lyons, *Assignment in Utopia*, 281.

47 'Valuta shops, valuta': Ibid., 451.

47 'The miracle of white': Ibid., 447.

49 'You believe that reality': Orwell, *1984*, 261.

50 'The party seeks': Ibid., 275, 277, 280.

51 'Good Lord, what': Fyodor Dostoevsky, *Notes from Underground*, trans. and ed. Michael R. Katz, New York and London, W. W. Norton, 2001, 10.

53 'Where the lives': Sebastian Haffner, *The Meaning of Hitler*, trans. Ewald Osers, London, Phoenix, 1979, 38–9.

55 'It is said': Sebastian Haffner, *Defying Hitler*, trans. Oliver Pretzel, London, Phoenix, 2002, 336.

55 'European history knows': Ibid., 104.

58 'I see in it': Alexander Herzen, *From the Other Shore*, Oxford, Oxford University Press, 1979, 108–9.

60 'History has developed': Alexander Herzen, *My Past and Thoughts*, Berkeley, Los Angeles and London, University of California Press, 1982, 507, 519, 521.

61 'horrified by the': Ibid., 460, 463.

63 'Just before the': Adam Fergusson, *When Money Dies: The Nightmare of the Weimar Hyper-Inflation*, London, Old Street Publishing, 2010, 1, 21, 25, 141, 181–2, 39.

68 According to some historians: W. Scheidel and S. J. Friesen, 'The Size of the Economy and the Distribution of Income in the Roman Empire', *Journal of Roman Studies*, vol. 99, 2009, 61–91.

74 'Suppose an individual': Leon Festinger, Henry W. Riecken and Stanley Schacter, *When Prophecy Fails*, Radford, Va, 2011, 3–4, 6–7.

74 'though for us': Frank Kermode, *The Sense of an Ending*, New York, Oxford University Press, 2nd edn, 2000, 6.

74 'The shadow of apocalypse': See John Gray, *Black Mass: Apocalyptic Religion and the Death of Utopia*, London, Penguin Books, 2007, 4–20.

CHAPTER 2: BEYOND THE LAST THOUGHT

83 'The chief defect': *Letters of Wallace Stevens*, ed. Holly Stevens, Berkeley and London, University of California Press, 1996, 449.

85 It would not be: See Philip Rieff, *The Mind of the Moralist*, 3rd edn, Chicago and London, University of Chicago Press, 1979, 17.

85 'I have set': Seneca, Epistle 51, *Epistles 1–65*, trans. R. M. Grummere, Cambridge, Mass. and London, Harvard University Press, 2002, 341.

87 'Your analysis suffers': Letter to Oskar Pfister cited by Philip Rieff, *The Triumph of the Therapeutic: Uses of Faith after Freud*, Wilmington, Del., ISI Books, 2006, 91.

88 'Probably very few': Sigmund Freud, 'A Difficulty in the Path of Psychoanalysis' (1917), *Complete Psychological Works*, Standard Edition, vol. 17, London, Vintage Classics, 2001, 143–4.

90 'Where id was': Sigmund Freud, 'New Introductory Lectures on Psychoanalysis' (1932–3), Lecture XXXI, *Complete Psychological Works*, vol. 22, 80.

91 'to live and work': See Mark Edmundson, *The Death of Sigmund Freud: Fascism, Psychoanalysis and the Rise of Fundamentalism*, London, Bloomsbury, 2007, 121–2,

and Peter Gay, *Freud: A Life for our Time*, London, Macmillan, 1988, 628.

92 'It may perhaps?': Sigmund Freud, 'Why War?' (1932), *Complete Psychological Works*, vol. 22, 211–12.

93 'These new myths': George Santayana, 'A Long Way Round to Nirvana', *The Philosophy of Santayana*, ed. Irwin Edman, New York, Charles Scribner's Sons, 1936, 576, 579, 580.

95 'the suggestion conveyed': Ibid., 574–5.

98 'An illusion is not': Sigmund Freud, *The Future of an Illusion*, trans. J. A. Underwood and Shaun Whiteside, London, Penguin Books, 2004, 38–9.

99 'there are plenty': Ibid., 34.

100 'No, our science': Ibid., 72.

101 'It has been said': The view that myths are degenerate fictions is argued in Frank Kermode, *The Sense of an Ending*, 2nd edn, New York, Oxford University Press, 2000, ch. II.

101 'We must indicate': H. Vaihinger, *The Philosophy of 'As If': A System of the Theoretical, Practical and Religious Fictions of Mankind*, trans. C. K. Ogden, London, Routledge, 2001, 81. Assisting with the first translation into English of Wittgenstein's *Tractatus* and producing in 1932 a translation into Basic English of James Joyce's *Finnegans Wake*, Ogden was the author of *Bentham's Theory of Fictions* (1932) and (with the literary critic I. A. Richards) *The Meaning of Meaning* (1923).

104 'The final belief': Wallace Stevens, *Opus Posthumous*, New York, Vintage Books, 1989, 189.

105 'It must / Be possible': Wallace Stevens, 'Notes toward

a Supreme Fiction', *The Palm at the End of the Mind*, ed. Holly Stevens, New York, Vintage Books, 1990, 230.

105 'a point / Beyond': Ibid., 229.

106 'to stick to': Wallace Stevens, 'The Pure Good of Theory', *The Palm at the End of the Mind*, 267–8.

107 'at the end': Wallace Stevens, 'Of Mere Being', *The Palm at the End of the Mind*, 398.

108 'I do not doubt': Sigmund Freud and Joseph Breuer, *Studies in Hysteria*, trans. Nicola Luckhurst, London, Penguin Books, 2004, 306.

110 'The ideal condition': Freud, 'Why War?', 213.

110 'A talent for': John Ashbery, 'Life Is a Dream', *Your Name Here*, Manchester, Carcanet, 2000, 59.

112 'In the realm': Sigmund Freud, 'Our Attitude towards Death', *Complete Works of Sigmund Freud*, vol. XIV, London, Vintage/Hogarth Press, 2001, 291.

115 'The Aryan unconscious': Edmundson, *The Death of Sigmund Freud*, 44.

116 Most likely the full truth: On this period in Jung's life, see Deirdre Blair, *Jung: A Biography*, New York, Little, Brown, 2003, 486–5; Peter Grose, *Allen Dulles: Spymaster*, London, André Deutsch, 2006, 164–5; Mary Bancroft, *Autobiography of a Spy*, New York, William Morrow, 1983, 91–7.

116 'But you mustn't': Richard Noll, *The Jung Cult: Origins of a Charismatic Movement*, London and New York, Free Press, 1997, 189.

118 'Looking out from': J. G. Ballard, *The Drowned World*, London, Indigo, 1997, 7, 19.

120 'The old men': Richard Jefferies, *After London: Wild England*, Oxford, Oxford University Press, 1980, 1.

122 '27th day. Have': Ballard, *The Drowned World*, 175.

122 'the silent gaming': J. G. Ballard, *Miracles of Life*, London, Fourth Estate, 2008, 58–9.

130 'I think of things': J. L. Borges, 'Things that Might Have Been', *Selected Poems*, London, Penguin, 1999, 407.

132 'Never think in': T. E. Hulme, 'Cinders', *Selected Writings*, ed. Patrick McGuinness, Manchester, Fyfield Books, 2003, 26.

133 'The truth is': Ibid., 29.

133 'Man is the chaos': Ibid., 24, 20, 22, 23, 24.

134 'put shortly, these': Hulme, 'Romanticism and Classicism', *Selected Writings*, 70.

136 'The great aim': Ibid., 78.

137 'A touch of cold': Hulme, 'Autumn', *Selected Writings*, 1.

137 'It's curious to': T. E. Hulme, 'Diary from the Trenches', *Further Speculations*, ed. S. Hynes, Lincoln, Nebr., University of Nebraska Press, 1955, 157.

138 'All I urge': Hulme, 'North Staffs Continues Where He Left Off', *Further Speculations*, 199.

138 Hulme's afterthought was: I am indebted to Patrick McGuinness's Introduction to Hulme's *Selected Writings*, pp. vii–xlv, for my knowledge of Hulme's life.

138 'I shall attempt': Fritz Mauthner, quoted in Gershon Weiler, *Mauthner's Critique of Language*, Cambridge, Cambridge University Press, 1970, 295.

139 'All philosophy is': L. Wittgenstein, *Tractatus Logico-Philosophicus* (1921; English translation, 1922), 4.0031.

140 When Wittgenstein compared: Weiler, *Mauthner's Critique of Language*, 298–9.

141 'For me it came': Quoted by Matthew Feldman, *Beckett's Books: A Cultural History of Samuel Beckett's 'Interwar Notes'*, London and New York, Continuum, 2006, 126.

141 'we feel with': Quoted in ibid., 130.

142 'Pure critique is': Ibid., 144.

142 'the silence that': Samuel Beckett, *Disjecta: Miscellaneous Writings and a Dramatic Fragment*, ed. Ruby Cohn, London, Calder, 1983, 172.

142 'On the way': Feldman, *Beckett's Books*, 128.

142 'folly – folly for to': Samuel Beckett, 'what is the word', *Company, Ill Seen Ill Said, Worstward Ho, Stirrings Still*, ed. Dirk Van Hulle, London, Faber & Faber, 2009, 133–5.

143 'The need for': Quoted by Elizabeth Bredeck, *Metaphors of Knowledge: Language and Thought in Mauthner's Critique*, Detroit, Wayne State University Press, 1992, 99.

145 'just in order': Weiler, *Mauthner's Critique of Language*, 294.

146 'The sands are': John Ashbery, 'The Skaters', *Collected Poems 1956–1987*, New York, Library of America, 2008, 175.

CHAPTER 3: ANOTHER SUNLIGHT

147 'The prevalence of': John Ashbery, 'As One Put Drunk into the Packet-Boat', *Self-Portrait in a Convex Mirror: Poems by John Ashbery*, Manchester, Carcanet, 2007, 2.

147 'The air is cool': J. A. Baker, *The Peregrine, The Hill of Summer and Diaries: The Complete Works of J. A. Baker*, introduced by Mark Cocker and edited by John Fanshawe, London, Collins, 2011, 237. I owe my knowledge of Baker's life to the account that has been pieced together by Cocker and Fanshawe in the Introduction and Notes to this book.

148 'For ten years': Ibid., 28, 31, 48, 131–2, 92, 201, 32, 128, 45–6, 33, 193, 114–15, 109, 119, 28, 98, 172, 31, 207, 161, 31, 28.

157 'Another sunlight': Wallace Stevens, 'As at a Theatre', *The Palm at the End of the Mind*, ed. Holly Stevens, New York, Vintage Books, 1990, 361.

158 'They emerge in': Patrick Leigh Fermor, *A Time to Keep Silence*, London, Penguin Books, 1982, 8–9. A brilliantly revelatory account of Leigh Fermor's life can be found in Artemis Cooper, *Patrick Leigh Fermor: An Adventure*, London, John Murray, 2012.

161 'I have often': Blaise Pascal, *Pensées*, ed. A. J. Krailsheimer, London, Penguin Books, 1966, 67.

161 'Men who are': Ibid., 68.

162 'The silence of': Max Picard, *The World of Silence*, South Bend, Ind., Regnery/Gateway, 111.

164 'We come from': Don Paterson, 'Phantom IV', *Rain*, London, Faber & Faber, 2009, 55.

166 'Attending there let': William Empson, *The Complete Poems*, ed. John Haffenden, London, Penguin Books, 2001, 55.

167 'To them the building': Richard Jefferies, 'The Pigeons at the British Museum', *The Life of the Fields*, Oxford and New York, Oxford University Press, 1983, 215–16.

169 'I have known': Ford Madox Ford, *The Soul of London*, London, Everyman/J. M. Dent, 1995, 23.

171 'Now that is no': Ford Madox Ford, 'On Impressionism', *The Good Soldier*, New York and London, W. W. Norton, 1995, 262–3.

173 'Thought of from': Ford, *The Soul of London*, 7.

175 'Though it has': Llewelyn Powys, 'A Pond', *Earth Memories*, Bristol, Redcliffe Press, 1983, 37–40.

176 'The shock of': Llewelyn Powys, *Skin for Skin*, London, Village Press, 1975, 5, 8, 9.

178 'I had done this': Ibid., 26.

179 'The possible annihilation': Llewelyn Powys, *Impassioned Clay*, London and New York, Longmans, Green, 1931, 4.

179 'It is not only': Llewelyn Powys, *Glory of Life*, London, Village Press, 1975, 27.

180 'Let it go': Powys, *Impassioned Clay*, 83–4.

180 'dream cattle, images': Powys, *Glory of Life*, 44.

181 'Sometimes, of an': Powys, *Skin for Skin*, 95.

181 'Well, I'll be': Ibid., 47.

182 'Adfrica, like one': Llewelyn Powys, *Ebony and Ivory*, Bristol, Redcliffe Press, 1983, 33.

183 'With a feeling': Llewelyn Powys, *The Verdict of Bridlegoose*, London, Village Press, 1975, 65–6.

184 'Presently I realized': Llewelyn Powys, *Love and Death*, London, John Lane/The Bodley Head, 1939, 301.

184 'Our origin is': Alyse Gregory, *The Cry of a Gull: Journals 1923–48*, Dulverton, Somerset, The Ark Press, 1973, 91, 105.

185 'They are dragging': Malcolm Elwin, *The Life of Llewelyn Powys*, John Lane/The Bodley Head, 1946, 271.

185 'I have had': See Anthony Head, Introduction to Llewelyn Powys, *A Struggle for Life: Selected Essays of Llewelyn Powys*, London, Oneworld Classics, 2010, ix.

185 'Immortal? . . . No': F. S. Flint, 'Immortal? . . . No', *Imagist Poetry: An Anthology*, ed. Bob Blaisdell, New York, Dover Publications, 1999, 44–5.

186 'had laid all ghosts': Georges Simenon, *M. Monde Vanishes*, in *The First Simenon Omnibus*, London, Penguin Books, 1975, 122, 20, 34, 87, 74, 110, 89.

193 'The laws of memory': Samuel Beckett, *Proust and Three Dialogues with Georges Duthuit*, London, John Calder, 1999, 18–19.

195 'the image of': Friedrich Nietzsche, *The Birth of Tragedy*, trans. Douglas Smith, Oxford, Oxford University Press, 2000, 83, 82.

196 'Not like a beast': Robinson Jeffers, 'The Humanist's Tragedy', *Rock and Hawk*, ed. R. Hass, New York, Random House, 1987, 115–18.

199 'a shifting of': Robinson Jeffers, 'Preface', *The Double Axe and Other Poems*, New York, Liveright, 1977, xxi.

199 'the devaluation of': Robinson Jeffers, 'Original Preface', *The Double Axe and Other Poems*, 171, 175.

200 'even the P-38s': Robinson Jeffers, 'Calm and Full the Ocean', *The Double Axe and Other Poems*, 125.

201 'was a religious': Czesław Miłosz, *Visions from San Francisco Bay*, New York, Farrar Straus & Giroux, 1982, 91.

202 'The earth teaches': Miłosz, 'To Robinson Jeffers', ibid., 96.

204 'My friend from': Robinson Jeffers, 'Credo', *Rock and Hawk*, 67.

206 'With my whole': Wallace Stevens, 'A Dish of Peaches in Russia', *Selected Poems*, ed. John N. Serio, New York, Alfred A. Knopf, 2009, 129.

208 'If there has been': Louis MacNeice, 'Mutations', *Collected Poems*, London, Faber & Faber, 2002, 195. I am grateful to Richard Holloway for drawing my attention to this poem, part of which appears in his book *Leaving Alexandria: A Memoir of Faith and Doubt*, Edinburgh and London, Canongate, 2012, 234-5.

Permissions